# Dynamic Flexibility:
# Train Your Body to Move

## ROD MURRAY, EP-C, CIFT, LMT, RYT

Developmental Editor: Susan Jankowitz, MA, EJD

P. Publishing
Morristown, NJ 07960 USA


*Cover photo* by Rebecca P. Feldman
*Cover photo* edit by Dave Walters, Big City Design
*Cover* by Glenn Jankowitz

ISBN 978-1080517992

# Client Testimonials

"I have been working with Rod Murray for the last four years at Body4Life. I started with dynamic flexibility classes to help me jump start my fitness journey. Rod is knowledgeable, caring, and an excellent professional. He has tailored my fitness plan according to my capabilities and my goals. About a year ago, I had an accident and broke my left arm. Fortunately, Coach Rod was able to continue working with me, which enabled me to fully recover within just a few months. I can honestly say that I am stronger than before. I owe this to Rod's workout plans, and his consistent encouragement and support."

—Angela Echeverri

"I am a 15-year-old cyclist who has been mountain bike racing for three years and cyclocross racing for two years. Recently, some back problems have risen while racing cyclocross. My back had gotten so bad that I even had to drop out of a couple races. I did not know what to do, when someone recommended Rod Murray at Body4Life. I started sessions there to work on my back. After just a few sessions, I noticed an incredible improvement when riding in both cyclocross and mountain biking. I am really glad Rod has helped me in my cycling career and am really happy with the results!"

—Sammy Morris
2019 National Interscholastic Cycling Association (NICA) NJ
Junior Varsity Girls State Mountain Bike Champion

"Rod Murray's approach to training, whole body wellness, and focus on dynamic flexibility has been the mainstay of my weekly workout sessions for the past 20 years. He is an expert in the truest sense. Rod continues to develop expertise with a long list of accreditations and certifications, ensuring that he is staying on the front line of training and coaching."

—Donna Babcock

"In 2000, I was diagnosed with bone cancer. I underwent limb salvage surgery, wherein bone was replaced by a prosthesis. After therapy, it had been a challenge to find an activity that would not exacerbate my disability and also improve my mobility. In my search to find an experienced exercise physiologist with the certifications to work with people with disabilities, I found Body4Life owner Rod Murray. I have been following Rod's dynamic flexibility regimen, which has been conducive to an increase in strength and flexibility without the propensity for injury. This has been the ideal routine to sustain longevity of my prosthesis, while allowing me to reach my strength and mobility goals. I highly recommend it."

—Rebecca Garcia
U.S. Army Disabled Veteran

"Honestly, dynamic flexibility has changed my life. Being a competitive cyclist for over 20 years has resulted in my body being inflexible. Dynamic flexibility has made me not only more flexible, but more powerful, healthier, and, best of all, happier!"

—Jesse Epstein
Owner, Marty's Reliable Cycle

"I was in my 50s, which was way too young to be waking up with back pain, hip pain, and still sluggish from a sleepless night. I knew I needed to focus more on my health. I began working with Rod, who introduced me to dynamic flexibility. Within just a few short weeks, the morning pain was almost gone, my balance had improved, and my energy level was higher. In fact, I took a ski trip out West—that I had previously been apprehensive about—and skied the best I had in years. Now, many years later, my dynamic flexibility workout is an integral part of my daily routine. What a difference! I'm more involved in outdoor activities and am stronger and more flexible. My endurance level is higher, and I am enjoying a happier, healthier quality of life than ever before."

—Lucille Deutsch, CALA, CMC
President, LHD Eldercare Solutions, LLC

"DFLEX has increased my balance and core and strength better than any other workout plan I've tried before. Lower back pain is now a thing of the past!"

—Alan J. Meltzer, MD, FAAP, Pediatrician
Director, General Pediatrics Goryeb Children's Hospital, Atlantic Health System

"After years of marathon running, I became plagued with injuries. Various back and hip problems would prevent me from running for weeks at a time. Since I began the dynamic flexibility routine, I have had practically no injuries and feel like my overall health has improved significantly."

—Heather McDermott
The Running Realtor, President of Super Hero events

"For me DFLEX has been fun, challenging, and has changed both the way my body works and how I feel about it. More coordinated, balanced, flexible and resilient. The gains have been quick and I enjoy all my other activities more, thanks to DFLEX a couple of times a week. It makes me feel younger."

—Rebecca Feldman
Smart Communities Proposal Manager, Verizon
Past President, Morristown Council

"Dynamic flexibility has been a great way to strengthen and stabilize my core. I leave feeling rejuvenated and ready to continue other programs, rather than beaten up and having to nurse aching muscles for days."

—Karla Doremus-Tranfield, US Air Force Academy Graduate
Business owner, mother of three and weekend endurance athlete!

"I have worked with Rod for nearly 25 years. Dynamic flexibility has been part of our regular workout routines. As a high school soccer coach, I was able to implement many of these exercises into daily practices and pre-game warmups. The benefits that both my players and I have reaped from incorporating these exercises have been innumerable. Dynamic flexibility has helped strengthen my core, improve and increase balance, reduce injury, and improve my overall physical fitness. I highly recommend this program for anyone looking to take his or her workouts to the next level."

—Athena Borzeka, Director of Student Personnel Services
and Special Education at the Morris County School of Technology

"I started dynamic flexibility with Rod Murray shortly after undergoing surgery for benign kidney tumors. I wanted to do something to help me recover from surgery and to improve my overall fitness. I was used to walking 10–15,000 steps per day consistently, but had little overall strength or flexibility. DFLEX helped to strengthen my entire body, especially my upper body strength, which was virtually non-existent, as well as my core. I feel fit and toned and at the age of 65, I feel like I'm at least 20–25 years younger!"

—Debbie Gottsieben, School Library Media Specialist,
Adjunct Professor, and Patient Advocate

"Dynamic flexibility has been an integral part of my workout program for more than 20 years and has helped me keep my very active lifestyle. Dynamic flexibility has helped me improve my balance and flexibility, but most of all it has given me tremendous core strength. The beauty of dynamic flexibility is that it is a total body workout and can be done anywhere! No need for expensive gym memberships!"

—Debbie Williams, RN
Certified Holistic Health Coach

"I was referred to Rod by my chiropractor to help me manage my chronic lower back pain. Since being introduced to dynamic flexibility, my core and overall lower back strength have dramatically improved. I have evolved my fitness and feel stronger than ever. My friends have noticed my transformation."

—Kelli Babich
Senior Manager Business Transformation and Change
Mars Global Services

"I am a mother of three with what was once called an athletic build. I've always exercised with trainers and taken classes. Some of the workouts I did were with a trainer who was teaching me "so called" functional training. The half-hour sessions left me feeling like a wet noodle with that "good hurt" in every muscle of my body. However, I often ended up injured in some way, which was both painful and discouraging. My chiropractor recommended working with Rod Murray, whose methodology she thought was safe and sane. We started the warmup for the program he called dynamic flexibility. At first, the warmup took an hour and I didn't even break a sweat! I was skeptical and disappointed. However, I stayed with it and started to see real results. My body is more toned and I feel physically stronger. I have a lot more energy, which allows me to be more focused and accomplish more at home and work. While I have always exercised, I haven't always loved going to the gym. Now I look forward to my dynamic flexibility workouts because, for the first time in my adult life, I'm getting amazing benefits without putting undue stress on my body. I can take it anywhere I go because it doesn't require any equipment!"

—Nancy Hedinger, President, League of Women Voters of New Jersey

# Table of Contents

# Foreword

I am delighted to present *Dynamic Flexibility: Train Your Body to Move*. Let me begin by stating that I never thought of myself as an athlete, nor did I ever profess to be one. I had a love for cycling, however, and rode my bike whenever I could find the time.

When I was 25 years old, I was hit by a car while out on a ride. This experience was devastating; the accident not only abruptly ended my cycling activities, but also my passion for the sport.

Fast forward 20 years, I found myself thinking about riding again. I had required back and knee surgery, but was feeling good. I was also inspired by my children, who wanted to ride their bikes with me. I started by riding on rail trails, and slowly built up the confidence to ride on roads again. I enjoyed riding with my children and worked hard to regain my cycling proficiency. I was happy with the results and knew that I never wanted to lose the gains I had made by starting to ride again. What I realized, however, was that I had lost a lot of strength and flexibility over those 20 years. It was then that I decided to take charge of my complete fitness journey.

Enter Rod Murray and his foundational functional movement program. Dynamic flexibility has allowed me to not only maintain my regained fitness, but improve my overall flexibility and core strength. I no longer suffer from lower back pain. My shoulders have an improved range of motion. My knees are no longer a hindrance. The strength and tone of my core has significantly improved.

Now in my 7th decade, I owe a huge debt of gratitude to Rod and his uniquely designed program. It is easy to follow. From the self-assessment, through to the exercises themselves, you don't require fancy equipment or have to spend excessive amounts of time or money. What you need is the simple willingness to put some of life's energy into caring for yourself. As you go through this book, I know you will find it to be as valuable a tool as I have toward achieving your overall health and wellness goals.

Alan J. Meltzer MD, FAAP
Director, General Pediatrics
Goryeb Children's Hospital, Atlantic Health System
July 2019

ಜ ಡ

# Introduction

When I reflect on my journey as a health, wellness, and fitness professional, it is hard to believe that more than 35 years have passed. 35 years. A generation. For some, a lifetime. I am grateful and blessed to have been given this time to craft my life's career, and for the amazing path I find myself on. Getting here has not always been easy, but the rewards for helping people improve their lives convinces me that I have always been on the right track. My hope for you in this book is that you will use it to achieve, maintain, and enjoy better health, wellness, and foundational fitness for life.

Over the past decade or so, the fitness industry has undergone significant change. Technology, social media, emerging fitness trends, more programs for older adults, and the continued evolution of healthcare are fundamentally redesigning the lens through which we view fitness. I am happy to see the direction in which the industry is going, as it is aligning more with my functional movement-based approach to fitness. Bodyweight and functional fitness training have received more support and are now more popular and widely used. Not mere fads, this type of training also ranks among the top global fitness trends as presented by the American College of Sports Medicine.

*Dynamic Flexibility A Guide to Foundational Fitness* was published four years ago. Since then, my client experiences and continued education have shown me that the dynamic flexibility framework originally presented has progressed and should be shared. My work with clients has also made it clear that the positive innovation in this industry has created some confusion, which I felt compelled to address.

In *Dynamic Flexibility: Train Your Body to Move*, your basic knowledge of functional movement and fitness at the foundational level is significantly deepened. I have added the much-needed clarification between flexibility and mobility, and stability and balance. You will also find an updated assessment and program development method to improve the efficiency and effectiveness of your time spent training. My clients are now more invested in their own holistic fitness education. You need more knowledge about how your body works at the foundational level, and also the role this knowledge plays in your functional movement success.

Over the past several years, I have continued to vigorously pursue outstanding client results, as well as my own athletic goals and education. Having recently become a registered yoga instructor, this RYT® certification not only confirms, but has further enabled my functional movement fitness approach with clients. Being able to move well is at the heart of any fitness program, not just a foundational one. 200 hours of yoga training has certainly reinforced this, my core belief. You wouldn't think that I am writing this as a USA certified weightlifting coach, but I couldn't be more sure of myself. Dynamic flexibility has been the cornerstone of my success as a dedicated, *non-injured* athlete, coach, and now as a yogi.

I am not here to judge traditional machine and equipment-based programs. If your goal is the NFL, I'm not suggesting you bypass training with the push pull sled or blocking body shield. If you are hooked on your favorite barbells at the gym, you are no doubt a dedicated strength athlete. If your goal is to run a marathon, those miles on the treadmill will help you get there. And what gymnast doesn't rely on the vault, uneven parallel bars, and balance beam? What I *am* saying is that you can use dynamic flexibility to improve your sports-specific goals. If you are not an athlete, nor wish to become one, use dynamic flexibility simply to help you achieve fitness at the foundational level. DFLEX is functional fitness training that can be used by and benefit people of all ages. Dynamic flexibility is portable, practical, safe, and inexpensive. My sole goal is to share my approach, which is centered primarily on using the power of your own body to achieve foundational fitness and functional movement success. Why? Because it works.

Beginning with the next chapter, you will learn how dynamic flexibility can enhance your existing sports program or be the only one you will ever need.

There are six chapters in this book. Chapter 1 discusses dynamic flexibility and human functional movement at the foundational level. Chapter 2 contains the functional movement self-assessment to help you identify your limitations and weaknesses. The flow charts and accompanying quick reference sheets in this chapter will help you visualize your self-assessment process and record meaningful notes based on your results. Chapter 3 contains the foundational movement exercises you need to build a strong fitness foundation. Chapter 4 contains the dynamic flexibility exercises you can use in a variety of ways for the rest of your life. Chapter 5 contains the Assessment Express℠. Once you develop your dynamic flexibility profile and program, use the Assessment Express to help you streamline your continued assessments, progress, and results. Chapter 6 provides you with valuable tips and guidance for creating your own dynamic flexibility routines. Throughout the book, use the Notes pages to record information related to your own findings and revised goals.

I couldn't agree more with—or be happier about—the amazing progress that we are all making together. Finally!

To your health, wellness, and fitness. Dream to achieve!

—Rod Murray, EP-C, CIFT, LMT, RYT

# Chapter 1: What is Dynamic Flexibility?

ᔕ To be fit, you must be strong and flexible. ᔐ

Dynamic Flexibility is an efficient and powerful foundational fitness modality that can be used by most people, regardless of activity or fitness level. Dynamic flexibility employs controlled, purposeful movements that are designed to help you develop and enhance your flexibility, mobility, and build core strength, stability, and balance.

Dynamic flexibility (DFLEX) can be used as part of an exercise program, a functional movement assessment tool, or a standalone exercise routine. You can also use DFLEX to help offset the consequences of inactivity, an illness, or injury. Whether you are an elite athlete, a recreational weekend warrior, or simply want to move better, dynamic flexibility can help you build and improve your overall fitness.

Throughout your fitness journey, you'll see physical therapists, doctors, and health and fitness professionals using the terms dynamic flexibility, dynamic stretching, and dynamic mobility interchangeably. In the American College of Sports Medicine's official journal, *Medicine and Science in Sports and Exercise*, for example, dynamic stretching is described as a type of flexibility exercise that can improve flexibility.[1] USA Triathlon Hall of Fame Athlete and 2004 Athens Olympic Games Olympian Barb Lindquist applies the term dynamic mobility to drills that are also referred to as dynamic flexibility exercises. Barb uses these dynamic mobility drills[2] in her highly successful triathlon training clinics.

When used as a pre-workout warmup, dynamic flexibility can help boost athletic performance. In her article, "Dynamic Stretching," physiotherapist Janice Eveleigh writes, "Dynamic stretching exercises have been shown to improve performance when done before an activity that requires a lot of power, strength or speed."[3] Some examples of these activities are basketball, soccer, cycling, CrossFit®, gymnastics, running, golf, and swimming.

---

[1] Carol E. Garber et al., "Quantity and Quality of Exercise for Developing and Maintaining Cardiorespiratory, Musculoskeletal, and Neuromotor Fitness in Apparently Healthy Adults: Guidance for Prescribing Exercise," *Medicine and Science in Sports and Exercise* 43, no. 7 (2011): 1344, doi: 10.1249/MSS.0b013e318213fefb.
[2] Barb Lindquist, (2019) "Dynamic Mobility Drills" [Class Handout].
[3] Janice Eveleigh, "Dynamic Stretching," *Stretching-Exercises-Guide*, n.d., accessed April 29, 2019, http://www.stretching-exercises-guide.com/dynamic-stretching.html.

Dynamic flexibility functions as an assessment tool to help identify challenges with flexibility, mobility, stability, balance, and strength. In his book, *Athletic Body in Balance*, functional movement expert Gray Cook discusses the need to "create a map for personal physical conditioning." [4] Cook, who co-founded Functional Movement Systems, trains people all over the world on functional physical mobility and stability screening, assessing, and testing. His products include the Functional Movement Screen® and Selective Functional Movement Assessment®.

The beauty of dynamic flexibility as a standalone exercise protocol is that your DFLEX program can be custom-designed based on what works for *you*. Not unlike a computer software developer, you get to build your own program using inputs, attributes, and outcomes specific to *your* needs and goals. As you progress and as your goals evolve, your DFLEX program can easily and continuously be updated to accommodate your improvements. Most of my clients tell me that dynamic flexibility workouts are the mainstay of their functional movement and foundational fitness success.

# Understanding Basic Functional Movement

In simple terms, human movement refers to the study of how the human body works. Those who study human movement are interested in learning how we move, and the factors that limit and enhance our ability *to* move.

Human *functional* movement does not seem to be as clearly defined or broadly understood. Functional movement refers to the integration of your body's various structures with proper movement techniques to achieve synergy. Functional movement is also something that should be understood within the context of its intended purpose. While some may want to become better athletes, others may be recovering from injury or simply want to move better. No matter what your goals are, a basic knowledge of functional movement will help you better understand and use dynamic flexibility to your best advantage.

### Physical Components

Let's start by looking at several key physical components involved in our body's foundational functional movement.

### *Bones*

Our bones are made of living, active cells that grow, repair, and communicate with other parts of the body. Bones represent our supportive frame; without them, we would be unable to stand up or maintain our structure. Light but strong, bones have different shapes, strengths, compositions, and tasks. Bones form a strong layer around certain organs to protect them from harm. Bones also fit together via joints, which enable us to move.

---

[4] Gray Cook, *Athletic Body in Balance*, (Chicago: Human Kinetics, 2003), ix.

## Joints

Joints, also known as articulations, are the places where two bones intersect (articulate). Our joints provide mechanical support for and allow the various ways in which our bodies move.

In general terms, there are three main types of joints: immovable (fibrous), slightly movable (cartilaginous), and freely movable (synovial). Immovable joints are important for the body's protection and stability. Slightly movable joints provide bone support and also help reduce friction between bones. Freely movable (synovial) joints also prevent friction between the bones and allow for greater mobility. There are several types of synovial joints, which include the elbow, wrist, knee, hip, and shoulder.

## Ligaments, Tendons, and Fasciae

Joints are held in place by soft tissues. These tissues include ligaments, tendons, fasciae, and muscles. Ligaments are sturdy, slightly pliable connective tissues that connect bone directly to bone. Ligaments provide stability to a joint both during rest and movement.[5] Tendons are strong, fibrous connective tissues that connect muscle to bone to support proper functioning of the body. Fascia is a connective tissue that is present throughout the body. Fasciae also help stabilize and keep organs and muscles separate, but connected to one another. "The fascial system supports the human body in its vital functions."[6]

## Muscles

The muscle system consists of bands, or bundles of fibrous tissue with the ability to contract and relax, thus producing movement as well as support. All of our movements are performed by muscles. There are three kinds of muscle tissue: cardiac, smooth, and skeletal. Of these types, both cardiac and smooth are involuntary, meaning that their movement cannot be controlled consciously. The skeletal muscles, on the other hand, are within our voluntary control. Without them, there is nothing to pull the bones in different directions. Every time you move your body, you employ the functional power of your skeletal muscle system.

## Anatomical Positions

Throughout this book, you'll work with the positions of your body (also known as stances) and the directions in which it moves. In the standard anatomical description, the body is upright, directly facing forward with the feet flat and directed forward. The upper limbs are at the body's sides. The palms are facing forward, and the thumbs are pointed away from the body.

---

[5] Keith Bridewell, "Ligaments," SpineUniverse. Updated April 10, 2018, accessed May 1, 2019, https://www.spineuniverse.com/anatomy/ligaments.
[6] Bruno Bordoni and Marta Simonelli, "The Awareness of the Fascial System," *Cureus* 10, no. 10 (October 2018): e3397, doi:10.7759/cureus.3397.

If the anatomical position is face-down, the body is in the prone position. If the anatomical position is face-up, the body is in the supine position.

**Note**: In this book, the palms face the sides in the upright starting position. When performing dynamic flexibility, this is referred to as the standard starting position.

## Anatomical Planes and Movement Types

"If we want to describe motion of the human body, we need to identify the space on which that motion occurs."[7] In anatomy, imaginary planes are used to divide the body into sections of motion to help us understand and analyze our various functional movement patterns.

### *Sagittal, Transverse, and Frontal Planes*

In basic terms, the body is divided into three planes. The sagittal plane is vertical and divides the body into left and right. The transverse plane is horizontal and divides the body into top and bottom. The frontal plane is also vertical, and divides the body into front and back. The reality concerning these planes is that most of our movements do not occur within a single dimension. When we move, we are usually engaging two or more of these planes.

### *Flexion and Extension*

Flexion and extension refer to the movements that decrease and increase the angle between two body parts. During flexion, the bones move toward each other at a joint, decreasing its angle.[8] An example of flexion is when you bend your elbow. Other examples include walking, forward and backward lunges, and squats. Extension reverses the movement of flexion. When you stand up, for example, this movement causes the angle to increase. Flexion and extension occur in the sagittal plane.

There is also dorsiflexion and plantar flexion, which refer to flexion movements at the ankle. (Dorsiflexion also occurs at the wrist.) Dorsiflexion is the action of raising the foot in the dorsal, or upward, direction. During plantar flexion, the top of the foot points away from the leg, such as in the case of a ballet dancer standing on the tips of the toes.

### *Abduction and Adduction*

Abduction and adduction describe the type of movement in which a limb is moved away from or toward the midline, or center, of the body. During abduction, movement is away from the body. An example of abduction is when you raise your

---

[7] "The Planes of Motion," You Tube video, 3:19, "ACEfitness," December 7, 2016, https://www.youtube.com/watch?v=0SNnCr0-9AQ.

[8] Clair Davies, and Amber Davies, *The Trigger Point Therapy Workbook*, Third Edition, (Oakland: New Harbinger Publications, Inc., 2013), n.p.

arms out to the sides. During adduction, movement is toward the body. An example of adduction is when you bring those outstretched arms back down to your sides. Abduction and adduction occur in the frontal plane.

### *Internal and External Rotation*

Internal (medial) and external (lateral) rotation describe the rotational movements toward or away from the body. When you walk or run, your hips perform internal rotation with every step you take. An example of external rotation is the upper body DFLEX pattern W on page 87, in which the arms are bent and rotated away from the center of the body. When you throw a ball, you are rotating both internally and externally. Internal and external rotation are movements that occur in the transverse plane.

### *Protraction and Retraction*

Protraction and retraction movements are portrayed in this book as push/pull exercises. Protraction involves moving a part of the body forward, as shown in the Push/Pull Protraction exercise on page 89. Retraction is the reverse movement of protraction, in which the body part is pulled backward. In the Push/Pull Retraction movement on page 89, the models are pulling their arms and shoulders back to their starting position. Protraction and retraction movements occur in the transverse plane.

## Range of Motion

Range of motion (ROM) describes the full movement potential of a joint or body part. Joint range of motion refers to both the distance a joint can move and the direction in which it can move. The normal ROM level is specific to each joint type, which means that the degree of mobility varies in accordance with the joint's structure.

ROM is also affected by a joint's surrounding soft tissues, including the muscles, tendons, and ligaments. If there is injury to the soft tissues, for example, or if muscles are weak or shortened (tight), reduced range of motion can occur. The self-assessment in Chapter 2 will guide you through a variety of functional movement checks to help identify any range of motion limitations.

In the rehabilitative world, physical therapists typically perform ROM assessments as a result of surgery, or pain resulting from injury or everyday activities. The particular joint or body part of the individual is measured in degrees and compared to its normal values. For example, the knee should ideally be able to flex, or bend, to an angle of 130°.[9] It should also be able to extend so that it is completely straight.[10]

---

[9] Alex Moroz, "Physical Therapy (PT)," Merck Manual for the Professional. Updated June, 2017, accessed May 7, 2019, https://www.merckmanuals.com/professional/special-subjects/rehabilitation/physical-therapy-pt.
[10] Ibid.

If a therapist assesses an individual's knee whose ROM measurement is somewhat less than 130°, a limitation would likely be diagnosed.

To move effectively, you need to be able to move your joints through their normal ranges of motion. *You* are the quarterback of your body's team. The performance of your key ROM players—bones, soft tissues, muscles, and joints—is critical to your functional movement success.

## Flexibility and Mobility

Flexibility refers to the ability to bring a muscle to its end point, or, lengthen it.

Mobility, on the other hand, is the ability of a joint to move actively through its fully intended range of motion. This means that a specific joint can do what it is designed to do. In her American Council on Exercise (ACE) blog entry, "Joint Mobility and Stability," Nicole Thompson refers to this mobility as the range of uninhibited movement around a joint."[11]

So, when you think about it, flexibility and mobility are not the same. If you do not have good flexibility, you cannot perform a normal range of motion pattern. This means that if you cannot lengthen and shorten a muscle properly, the mobility of that joint will be affected; its movement will become inhibited. I believe that healthy functional movement at the foundational level—a key goal of dynamic flexibility—requires both flexibility and mobility.

## Balance and Stability

Although balance and stability are interchangeable and closely related, they are not the same thing. Balance and stability require control, but it is possible to have one and not the other.

Balance describes your ability to maintain an upright and steady position; you can control your body's center of mass over its base of support. Balance is a critical component of your body's normal functional movement. In anatomical terms, balance refers to the ability to maintain your body's center of mass over its base of support; it is about control. Balance is composed of three body systems: vision, proprioception (sense of where you are in space), and vestibular (inner part of the ear). In basic terms, you process the input from these systems to control your equilibrium, whether static (motionless or at rest) or dynamic (in motion). The Single Limb Balance test on page 50 is an example of static balance, which is the ability to maintain the body in a fixed position. A young toddler learning to walk is developing dynamic equilibrium, which is the ability to maintain the body's balance in motion.

---

[11] Nicole Thompson, "Joint Mobility and Stability," March 7, 2019, *American Council on Exercise* (blog), https://www.acefitness.org/fitness-certifications/ace-answers/exam-preparation-blog/1189/joint-mobility-and-stability.

When considering stability, there are several types of stability associated with foundational functional movement. Core stability relates to the ability to achieve and maintain control of the trunk area at rest and during movement. Postural stability is defined as the ability to maintain an upright position. Spinal stability can be related to the spinal cord and its ligaments, the muscles, and your nervous system, which controls spinal movement. Joint stability is defined as the ability to maintain or control joint movement or position.[12] Muscle, tendon, and ligament action are needed to hold a joint in its position. And as Thompson says, "Once the body parts are stable in the right spots and mobile in the right spots, we can teach the body to move".[13]

## Strength

In basic terms, strength is associated with muscle strength and refers to the ability of the body to exert force. Let's take it a step further; strength is the maximum or near maximum amount of force that a muscle can exert against resistance. This resistance can be in the form of weight machines, free weights, miscellaneous other equipment, or your own body weight.

There are several different types of strength. In his ACE blog entry, "7 Different Types of Strength and Their Benefits," Pete McCall writes, "To achieve a strength-based goal, it is important to first define the specific type of strength required for success and then design an exercise program to develop that strength."[14] Although this book is about using your own body weight as your best strength-building tool, the table below can be used for general reference.

| Strength Type | Description and Illustration |
|---|---|
| Absolute | <ul><li>Maximum amount of force you can produce for one all-out effort, regardless of your size or body weight</li><li>Deep Squats</li><li>Increases bone density and lean muscle mass</li></ul> |
| Agile | <ul><li>Ability to move and change direction of your body position while maintaining control (functional, mobile type of strength)</li><li>Picking up and moving a chair from your desk to another room, Floor Ladder Crawl</li><li>Improves daily functional movement, balance and stability, reduces risk of injury</li></ul> |
| Bodyweight | <ul><li>Uses your body as resistance against gravity</li><li>Basic abilities such as pushing, pulling, squatting, balancing, DFLEX</li><li>Improves mobility, strength, balance, stability, reduces risk of injury</li></ul> |

---

[12] Ibid.

[13] Ibid.

[14] Pete McCall, "7 Different Types of Strength and Their Benefits," June 29, 2015, *American Council on Exercise* (blog), https://www.acefitness.org/education-and-resources/professional/expert-articles/5495/7-different-types-of-strength-and-their-benefits.

| Strength Type | Description and Illustration |
|---|---|
| Endurance | ▪ Ability to maintain muscular contractions or a consistent level of muscle force for extended periods of time<br>▪ Running a 10k, dynamic exercises in this book<br>▪ Improves aerobic capacity of working muscles and ability to perform many functional tasks[15] |
| Explosive | ▪ Ability to exert maximal force in minimal time (acceleration or rate of force development)<br>▪ Working with barbells, throwing a shot-put<br>▪ Improves the resiliency of muscle and connective tissue[16]<br>▪ Component of speed strength |
| Maximum | ▪ Measure of how much force your body can exert<br>▪ Bench presses<br>▪ Increases muscle, tendon, and ligament strength, builds postural support |
| Reactive | ▪ Ability to absorb force in one direction and then apply greater force in the opposite direction<br>▪ Vertical jumping (movement in which one jumps vertically off the ground from an upright standing position)<br>▪ Promotes speed in execution of movement |
| Relative | ▪ How strong you are in relation to your body size<br>▪ Gymnastics movements<br>▪ Promotes functional movement efficiency and reduced fatigue |
| Speed | ▪ Maximum force capable of being produced during a high-speed movement<br>▪ Running sprint starts, shot put, emergency situation, such as quickly moving out of the way to avoid a car<br>▪ Strengthens bones and other connective tissues |
| Starting | ▪ Ability to produce force at the beginning of a movement without momentum<br>▪ Javelin throw, running sprint starts<br>▪ Component of speed strength |

As explained in the *Muscles* section, each muscle is made up of fibers that contract and relax. When muscle fibers contract, they shorten the muscle and move the bone the muscle attaches to via the tendon. Simply put, your muscles are what allow you to move.

The size of the muscle and the number of fibers that contract determine how much force a muscle can generate when it is asked to contract. There has to be a sufficient number of muscle fibers that are working well in order for your muscle to have the strength it needs to move your bone the way you want it to be moved. Walking down the street may be less strenuous than training for a marathon, but both require a certain amount of strength. The number of fibers asked to contract is controlled by the nervous system and your brain.

---

[15] Ibid.
[16] Ibid.

## Neurological Control

Movement of *any* kind is controlled by the brain. The brain sends a signal to your shoulder muscles and asks the muscles to contract in a specific order and at a specific intensity for you to lift your arm overhead. If you had a weight in your hand, the brain signal would be different. This is because your brain would already be calculating the fact that it takes more force to lift a weighted arm than an unweighted arm. This is just one example that shows the connection between your brain and your muscles must be strong and efficient for good functional movement to occur. It must be well calculated and coordinated.

A well-coordinated muscle does not need to be bulked up to work efficiently. If all of your muscle fibers are working together, even in a smaller muscle like your bicep, you can become incredibly strong without building a lot of bulk. When there is good neurological control and your muscle is strong, you will develop functional stability. Without good neurological control, having range of motion, flexibility, mobility, and strength will not be sufficient enough to give you normal movement.

## Comparing Static Stretching with Dynamic Flexibility

At a basic level, stretching can be broken down into two different types: dynamic and static.

### *Static Stretching*

Static stretching is the most common form of stretching you will find in a general fitness program and it is also used in Yoga and Pilates. When you perform a static stretch, you are reaching as far as you can until you start to feel uncomfortable and then holding the position. Static stretching has a long history of use in both the fitness and rehabilitative worlds.

Static stretching helps increase joint range of motion and muscle flexibility. If you have limited hip extension because your hip flexors are tight, you could be putting more strain on your back, your knees, or both while walking or running. Static stretching would be the appropriate way to treat the limited hip flexibility to improve your functional movement and reduce strain on your back and knees.

In several research studies, static stretching has been shown to *reduce* performance in athletes when used immediately prior to sports requiring explosive movements. Some examples of these sports include cycling, running, and football. One study examined the effects of static stretching versus dynamic stretching in young male soccer players. Results of the study showed that static stretching of the lower limbs and hip muscles before exercise had a negative impact on explosive performance for up to twenty-four hours.[17] This is not to say, however, that static stretching does not have several important benefits.[18]

An effective time to perform static stretching is actually after a workout, once your muscles and joints are warmed up. For those of us who are not blessed with natural flexibility, static stretching can help to lengthen the tissue structures and restore necessary functional movement.

### Dynamic Stretching

Dynamic stretching is the fluid motion from a full stretch in one direction, through mid-range to a full stretch in the other direction with one to dozens of repetitions. You are moving and reaching over and over again. In his article in the *International Journal of Sports Physical Therapy*, Fellow of the American College of Sports Medicine Dr. Phil Page describes dynamic stretching as "...moving a limb through its full range of motion to the end ranges and repeating several times...."[19]

Dynamic stretching describes what most of us do on a daily basis without thinking about it. It's functional. When you change a lightbulb, or when a basketball player reaches up to block a pass, dynamic stretching accomplishes the task. Reaching, stretching, or flowing from one position to another is a normal part of daily life.

Some research suggests that dynamic stretching exercises can be more useful for improving performance than other forms of stretching. In the New York Times bestseller, *The First 20 Minutes*, Gretchen Reynolds presents some of her research findings on both static and dynamic stretching.[20] Reynolds writes, "Dynamic stretching may be the most important, if often neglected, element of a proper warm-up."[21] Reynolds also recommends that a dynamic stretching routine follow light, easy aerobic exercise and be "relatively sports specific."[22]

Dynamic stretching should be part of a healthy, well-balanced exercise routine and is what largely makes up dynamic flexibility. Dynamic flexibility, however, expands on the strength and neurological components of movement. It is not possible to be foundationally fit without all the components of movement: ROM, flexibility, mobility, stability, balance, strength, and neurological control.

---

[17] Monoem, Haddad et al., "Static Stretching Can Impair Explosive Performance for at Least 24 Hours," *Journal of Strength and Conditioning Research*, no. 1 (January 2014): 3008.

[18] Ibid., 3008.

[19] Page, Phil, "Current Concepts in Muscle Stretching for Exercise and Rehabilitation," *International Journal of Sports Physical Therapy 7*, no. 1 (February 2012): 109–119.

[20] Gretchen Reynolds, "Stretching The Truth," in *The First 20 Minutes*, (New York: Penguin, 2013), 25-49.

[21] Ibid., 24.

[22] Ibid., 35.

### *Dynamic Flexibility for the Not-So-Flexible*

You don't need to be particularly flexible to benefit from dynamic flexibility, because the goal is not flexibility for its own sake. The goal is to be fit first—to develop a foundational level of fitness that enables you to function well with daily and recreational activities. That means that you only need to have enough flexibility to complete the task at hand. To tie your shoes, for example, you need a minimum amount of hip and knee flexibility. You need to get your foot closer to your body so that your hands can reach the laces.

Injuries don't occur simply from being inflexible. They can occur when you use the wrong body part to move. You need to be flexible *where* you need to move. If you are flexible through the range of motion that you need, then you probably don't need to spend countless hours trying to become more flexible. Developing flexibility for its own sake is not and should never be the final goal. Flexibility is foundational to good quality movement, of course, but only in the context of functionality.

A lot of people are not flexible where they need to be. To compensate for a lack of motion in one area, they overuse another. This is sometimes the cause of overuse and repetitive strain injuries such as tendonitis. In the next chapter, you will be able to determine what joints may lack range of motion or what muscles you may need to stretch. If you determine that you have a flexibility limitation, you can use the stretching exercises provided in Chapter 3 to address any of those limitations.

The process to change from being not-so-flexible to flexible represents a challenge for a lot of us. Depending on the research, some believe that flexibility is largely based on genetics and consistency. Others adamantly refute this claim. At the end of the day, some of us are Gumby (the American clay character), but many of us are more like Frankenstein's monster. If the latter seems to describe you, know that the monster will become more flexible with practice, but it will take considerable effort and time.

### *Dynamic Flexibility for the Flexible Yet Movement Challenged*

It is possible to have full joint ROM and full muscle flexibility, yet still be injury prone or have difficulty moving well. As you are learning in this book, functional fitness at the foundational level is multifaceted. Flexibility is only one component. You also need strength and good neurological control. If you have good flexibility but lack strength and neurological control, you will not be able to run, jump, or maybe even roll over in bed. Flexibility has to be balanced with functional strength and control to help create normal movement; the combination of these is functional stability.

Remember that the connection between your brain and muscles is intimate and that they work together to create functional stability. If this stability is limited, you may not be able to perform everyday tasks. Each movement in the next chapter introduces the possibility that there may be a stability limitation and not a flexibility limitation. An additional goal of the dynamic flexibility exercises in Chapter 4 is to help you develop and improve that stability. It takes time and effort to make changes toward improving functional movement, but the rewards are worth the work.

## Putting it Together

Each component discussed in this chapter is designed to interact with the other in order to create beautifully coordinated, strong, efficient functional movement patterns.

The exercises in this book integrate the essential elements of optimal functional movement with updated research in an enjoyable, easy to implement, challenging movement assessment and workout. The dynamic flexibility routines will fully move your joints and soft tissues through their respective ranges of motion and flexibility. DFLEX also promotes neurological control by way of purposeful and controlled motion. Dynamic flexibility will help you create a strong functional movement foundation that will also allow you to build toward more advanced physical skills.

Each movement in this book has a specific goal to test your fitness and help you achieve normal functional movement. No matter your fitness level, you should have a certain defined level of foundational functional fitness. You need some level of fitness to safely perform activities such as running, biking, tennis or golf, to name only a few examples. But you also need a certain level of fitness to carry a bag of groceries or mow your lawn. Dynamic flexibility helps you identify weak areas and gives you a plan to address them.

# Chapter 2: Functional Movement Self-Assessment

&infin; Personal responsibility means taking care of yourself so that
someone else won't have to. &infin;

I discussed in Chapter 1 that not everyone is naturally flexible, graceful, balanced, and coordinated. The truth is that many people have one or more functional movement limitations. These limitations include challenges with flexibility, range of motion (ROM), balance, strength, and postural stability.

The particular movements in this assessment section are designed to help you find those strengths and challenges. If you discover limitations in one or more of the movement patterns or specific joints, a list of suggested exercises is provided. Use this as a guide only. If you experience pain at *any* point during this assessment, stop immediately and consult your healthcare provider.

The goal of this functional movement tool is to provide you with a safe, effective, and logical self-assessment framework for understanding your specific movement patterns. Use this assessment to help determine the minimum flexibility, mobility, balance, ROM, strength, and postural stability you need to move well at the foundational level.

## Self-Assessment Guidelines

1.  Your muscles should be cold when you try these maneuvers. Cold muscles will provide a more accurate baseline measure of you at your most natural, normal state. (Warm up before exercise and sports, but *not* for this assessment.)

2.  Perform the assessment without shoes. Most shoes are made with a slight heel, even tennis shoes and sneakers. Having a lifted heel puts your foot in what's called a plantar flexed position, which shortens your heel cord. If you wear shoes, you will think you have better movement patterns than you really do.

3.  If a movement is painful, stop immediately! These movements are designed to help you find your weak spots, but none of them should ever hurt. *Ever!* If you experience pain at any point, stop right away and have the problem area evaluated by your healthcare provider.

4.  If you can't do a movement, there could be one or more things wrong that are limiting you. You may have a tight or weak muscle, ligament, tendon, or other limitation such as postural instability. If you experience a limitation with a movement, note it in the appropriate quick reference sheet.

5. Give yourself three attempts per movement. If you can't do a specific movement within three attempts, it means that you have identified your limitation. Continuing to practice the movements will skew the result of the test because your body will adjust to meet the demands placed on it.

6. Use the best form you can! If you can't do a particular maneuver using good form, accept that there is a limitation of some kind and move on to the next movement.

7. You should reach the end of the movements, but do not force or strain them.

8. Enlist the help of someone who can watch and critique you as you perform your self-assessment. A second pair of eyes may pick out the finer points of the movement you might miss by doing it yourself.

9. Complete the entire assessment! Because some limitations correspond with others, you will notice some overlap in the self-assessment movements. For example, shoulder range of motion limitations often correlate to limitations of the upper back. Use the flow charts provided to help guide you through the assessment.

10. If you are able to perform the first movement in a section without difficulty, there is no need to do the sub-movements provided. The first movement is the most important. The sub-movements are designed to help you further determine where your limitation is coming from.

11. Use the quick reference sheets to keep a record of your challenges. By doing so, you'll have a much better picture of where you need to focus your training efforts.

12. Once you identify your limitations, you are directed to the appropriate exercises. Range of motion and flexibility limitations should be addressed first. Follow them with the appropriate stability exercises. Initially, you may need to perform this combination 1–2 times daily to restore normal movement. Once you are moving normally, you will only need to do the exercises outlined in Chapter 4.

## Using the Self-Assessment Flow Charts and Quick Reference Sheets

There are six visual charts in the chapter. These charts provide you with a quick overview of each assessment. Although they may seem a little intimidating at first, their design is simple and easy to follow. Each chart has a corresponding quick reference sheet for you to record your notes.

You can find these materials after each of the following assessments: neck, upper back, lower back, whole body extension, whole body flexion, and squatting.

You'll notice that these charts and quick reference sheets contain more, not less, information. If a chart or reference sheet exercise category offers an extensive list of exercises, it does *not* mean you have to perform every one! Go at your own pace and do only what you comfortably can. Remember that you want to strive for progress, not perfection.

# Defining Good Posture

Most of us have heard our mothers tell us to sit up straight. In fact, there is a lot of truth to good posture being important for our health. Having good posture decreases the strain on your muscles during functional activities, as well as in resting positions like sitting and standing. The following is a description of good posture.

The spine should have a natural S-shaped curve with the head balanced on top in the midline. A simple plumb line dropped from the ceiling is enough to give you a visual cue as to what good posture should be.[1]

From the side view, your ear, shoulder, hip (greater trochanter), middle of your knee, and front of your ankle should all be in line. From the front view, your chin should be in line with the midline of your body, essentially bisecting you into two equal halves. Your shoulders, pelvis, and knees should be level and parallel to the floor.

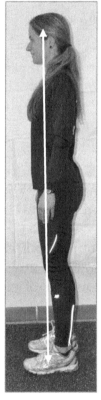

Ch. 2 Fig. 1. Side View

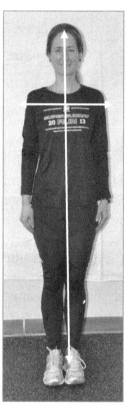

Ch. 2 Fig. 2. Front View

**Note**: Not everyone is perfectly symmetrical, but you should be fairly close to symmetrical.

---

[1] Florence P. Kendall. Muscles: Testing and Function. (Baltimore: Williams and Wilkins, 1983), p. 19.

## Neck Flexion

The head houses the brain, but without a neck to move and hold up the head, our brains wouldn't be nearly as useful. Begin by standing in an upright position with both feet flat on the floor and close together—touching if possible. Start with a level chin and then look down as though you are trying to touch your chin to your chest. Keep your mouth gently closed during this neck flexion movement.

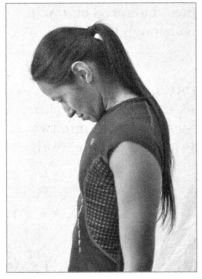

Ch. 2 Fig. 3. Neck Flexion

Key points of a normal Neck Flexion test:

- ✔ Your chin should be able to touch your chest or be less than one finger-width from your chest.
- ✔ Your neck and upper back should be evenly rounded.

If you cannot touch your chin to your chest, you likely have some restriction in your muscles, vertebral joints, or both. The limitation could be in your neck or upper back.

*Exercises to Increase Neck Flexion*

Chin Tuck p. 55

Chin Tuck and Roll p. 58

Levator Stretch p. 58

## Neck Rotation

While being able to look down is important, looking side to side is even more important. You need to look both ways when you cross the street. You need to check your blind spots when you are driving. Turning your head is a vital function.

According to the data available, normal neck rotation should be approximately 70–80 degrees of rotation. What does that mean? You should be able to turn your head to the side and your chin should be in line with the middle of your collarbone. Your chin should be able to touch your collarbone.

To assess your neck rotation, start by standing with your feet together and flat on the floor. Turn your head to the right as far as you can, then gently tip your chin downward as if you are trying to touch your chin to your collarbone. Now turn your head to the left as far as you can, and then gently tip your chin downward in the same manner. Do not elevate your shoulder to meet your chin. This movement is easiest to assess when someone is helping you out but it can be done in front of a mirror.

Ch. 2 Fig. 4. Neck Rotation

Key points of a normal Neck Rotation test:

✔ Your chin should be in line with the last third of your collarbone.

✔ There should be symmetrical motion of the neck in both directions.

Sometimes there is a postural problem that limits neck rotation. If you cannot turn your chin all the way, try adjusting your posture to be fully erect with your ear, shoulder, hip, and ankle all in one line. If you can fully rotate your neck after having made this adjustment, your posture might have been the issue.

You will need to focus on postural stability exercises to reduce any limitations in neck rotation. If your range of motion does not increase with improved posture, you likely have restrictions in your muscles or vertebral joints that are limiting your motion.

*Exercises to Increase Neck Rotation*

Chin Tuck and Rotate p. 56

Levator Stretch p. 58

Scalene Stretch p. 59

*Postural Stability Exercises*

Lumbar Locked Rotation p. 62

Quadruped Alternating Extension p. 73

Front Planks/Side Planks p. 74

Upper Body Dynamic Flexibility Patterns pp. 86–88

## Neck Extension

Most people don't spend a lot of time looking up, but being able to look up is important in many common situations. What if you need to change a lightbulb? Reach up into a storage space? Ride a road bike? At some point, everyone needs to look up.

While the neck supports the head, it also houses vital components of our vasculature (arteries) and the brain stem, which controls breathing and other vital functions.

**Caution**: Looking up can cause dizziness or lightheadedness in some people. If you experience these symptoms, *stop* and consult your healthcare provider.

Begin the test by standing flat on the floor with your feet together and your hands at your sides. Look up as far as possible. In a normal range of motion for looking up, your forehead should be parallel to the floor. This exercise is best performed with someone who can help gauge your range of motion. If you are not able to look up fully, the same neck rotation concept applies: there might be a postural stability issue. Keep in mind that your neck is a very delicate structure in many respects. Neck extension is often difficult to perform.

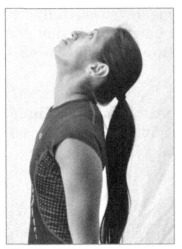

Ch. 2 Fig. 5. Neck Extension

*Exercises to Increase Neck Extension*

Chin Tuck and Extend p. 57

Scalene Stretch p. 59

Foam Roller Thoracic Spine Extension p. 59

If you have a problem with looking upward or encounter tightness issues with this movement, it's best to seek the help of a professional. A physical therapist or physician can more thoroughly evaluate the problem and help you with any limitations. If, however, there is no dizziness, pain, or other difficulty, you can work on stretching the front structures of the neck.

## Self-Assessment Flow Chart 1: The Neck

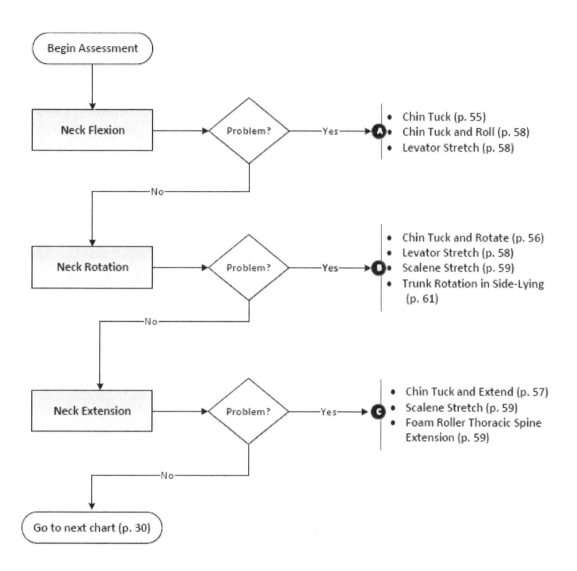

## Quick Reference Sheet 1: The Neck

Note any trouble spots you may have discovered in your neck assessment by putting a check next to the appropriate test name below. Proceed to the exercises provided in the right column. Record important notes in the space provided below.

| ✔ | Test Name | Category | Exercise Names |
|---|-----------|----------|----------------|
| | Neck Flexion | A | Chin Tuck (p. 55)<br>Chin Tuck and Roll (p. 58)<br>Levator Stretch (p. 58) |
| | Neck Rotation | B | Chin Tuck and Rotate (p. 56)<br>Levator Stretch (p. 58)<br>Scalene Stretch (p. 59)<br>Trunk Rotation in Side-Lying (p. 61) |
| | Neck Extension | C | Chin Tuck and Extend (p. 57)<br>Scalene Stretch (p. 59)<br>Foam Roller Thoracic Spine Extension (p. 59) |

**Notes:** ✎

_____

_____

_____

_____

_____

_____

_____

_____

_____

_____

_____

## Upper Extremity: Shoulder Complex

Your upper extremity consists of the shoulders, arms, forearms, wrists, and hands. There is rarely a time when we use only one joint in an upper extremity to complete a task. If you are a runner, for example, your arm has to swing from the shoulder and elbow to help generate momentum. If you are washing dishes, you have to use your shoulders to stabilize the rest of your arms so your elbows can bend and your hands can wash. Each whole arm works as a unit. Even if you are doing something simple such as writing or typing, you need to use your shoulders. The shoulders stabilize the arms so you can complete the task.

All upper extremity movement is assessed as a unit with several different patterns that maximize the motion in each joint.

## Movement One: Upper Back Scratch Test

The following test is a combined movement of shoulder flexion, abduction (moving the arm out to the side), external rotation, and elbow flexion.

Standing with your feet flat on the floor and close together, reach one arm up and over your head to your upper back. Next, scratch the imaginary itch on your upper back. Perform this movement first on one side and then on the other.

Ch. 2 Fig. 6. Upper Back Scratch Standing Position

Key points of a normal Upper Back Scratch Test:

- ✔ Both hands should be able to reach symmetrical distances.
- ✔ Each hand should be able to touch at least the top edge of the shoulder blade (the spine of the scapula) on the opposite side.
- ✔ Each elbow should be pointed toward the ceiling.
- ✔ The shoulder blade should be flat against your rib cage.

- ✔ The head should remain in a neutral position (should not jut excessively forward to avoid the arm).
- ✔ The upper back should not round out.

If you can perform this test without difficulty, move on to Shoulder Movement Two: Lower Back Scratch Test on page 32.

If you encountered difficulty with this movement, you can break it down to determine the cause. The problem could be tightness in your shoulder, upper back, or a postural stability issue.

The first thing you want to rule out is a postural stability problem. Do the Upper Back Scratch Test again as a test, but this time lie on your stomach on a table. Try to position yourself so that your neck is as neutral as possible (face down without any rotation). Place your non-test hand under your forehead to keep the neck in a comfortable, neutral position. If you can now perform this movement without any difficulty, your standing posture may have been the problem. Postural stability limitations can also make it hard to raise the arm while standing. If you have this challenge, you will need to work on improving your postural stability.

*Postural Stability Exercises*

    Lumbar Locked Rotation p. 62

    Quadruped Alternating Extension p. 73

    Front Planks/Side Planks p. 74

    Upper Body Dynamic Flexibility Patterns pp. 86–88

Ch. 2 Fig. 7. Upper Back Scratch on Table

If you are still unable to do the movement, there may be a restriction in your shoulder or upper back. Proceed to the following Shoulder Complex Tests: Flexion and External Rotation, and Thoracic Spine Test: Rotation sections.

## Shoulder Complex Tests: Flexion and External Rotation

There are two components to keep in mind with the shoulder complex. The first is range of motion of the shoulder joint into flexion and external rotation. The second is shoulder strength and postural stability.

Start by checking to see if you have the strength and range of motion to perform shoulder flexion while lying on your stomach on a table. Place the non-test hand under your forehead to keep your neck in a neutral, comfortable position.

Raise your other arm straight out in front of you. If you are able to lift the arm straight out in front, your shoulder has full range of motion into flexion and the strength to do so.

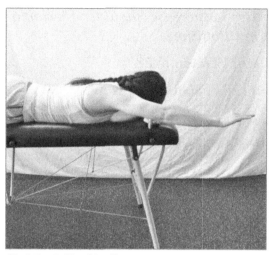

Ch. 2 Fig. 8. Shoulder Flexion

The next step is to check the external rotation component of the movement. This check is also done while lying on your stomach on a table.

Slide over a bit on the table so that your elbow is at the edge and your forearm is hanging perpendicular to the floor. Lift your hand, palm side toward the floor. Your forearm should now be parallel to the floor. You can place a towel under your elbow for comfort.

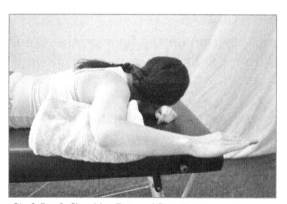

Ch. 2 Fig. 9. Shoulder External Rotation

If you are able to complete both the flexion and external rotation tests without any difficulty, you can rule out your shoulder as the limiting factor in completing the Upper Back Scratch Test. Move on to the Thoracic Spine Test: Rotation on page 28. However, if you have difficulty raising your arm into flexion, external rotation, or both, there is a limitation with range of motion, shoulder strength, or postural stability.

To determine if you have an issue with your range of motion, repeat the test lying on your back. If you are still unable to achieve full range of motion, you most likely have limitations in your shoulder joint or muscles that prevent full movement. The range of motion limitation needs to be addressed before focusing on any strength limitations of your shoulder muscles.

*Exercises to Increase Shoulder Flexion and External Rotation*

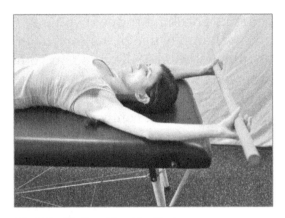

Levator Stretch p. 58

Pectoralis (Doorway) Stretch p. 60

Cane Shoulder Flexion p. 62

*Postural Stability Exercises*

Quadruped Alternating
Extension p. 73

Front Planks/Side Planks p. 74

Ch. 2 Fig. 10. Cane Shoulder Flexion

**Note**: As long as you do not experience pain, you can use these exercises to work on increasing your range of motion. If you experience catching sensations or a constant, dull, achy shoulder or other pain during any of these maneuvers, stop and consult your healthcare provider.

## Thoracic Spine Test: Rotation

Limitations in thoracic spine mobility can impact the normal movement patterns of your shoulder. To see if the limitation you discovered in the Upper Back Scratch Test on page 25 is coming from the upper back, perform the following test.

Get down onto your hands and knees into a crawl position on the floor or mat. Your hands are underneath the shoulders and knees under your hips. Now sit back on your heels.

Place your right elbow midline between your knees, but about 2–4 inches in front of them. Take your left hand and place your fingers by your ears or on your upper back. Keeping your butt down against your heels, try to look up toward the ceiling to the left. Repeat on the opposite side. This movement isolates motion to your thoracic spine. You should be able to rotate symmetrically, approximately halfway to vertical.

28

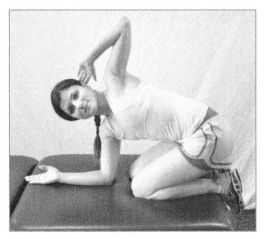

Ch. 2 Fig. 11. Thoracic Spine Rotation

Because of complex biomechanics, if you are limited with thoracic rotation, you will also be limited with thoracic extension. You need to be able to both rotate and extend to have been successful with the Upper Back Scratch Test on page 25. The exercises below will help you with both thoracic spine range of motion and postural stability.

*Exercises to Increase Thoracic Spine Motion*

Foam Roller Thoracic Spine Extension p. 59

Lumbar Locked Rotation p. 62

Once you have isolated whether most of your trouble is in the shoulder or thoracic spine, you can use that information to focus your exercise program. You should do the exercises that will help improve your limitation on a daily basis until your range of motion and strength increase. The objective is to be able to comfortably perform all of the functional movements without difficulty. By working toward this important goal, you are building a strong fitness foundation that will enhance nearly all of your activities.

## Self-Assessment Flow Chart 2: Upper Extremity Movement One

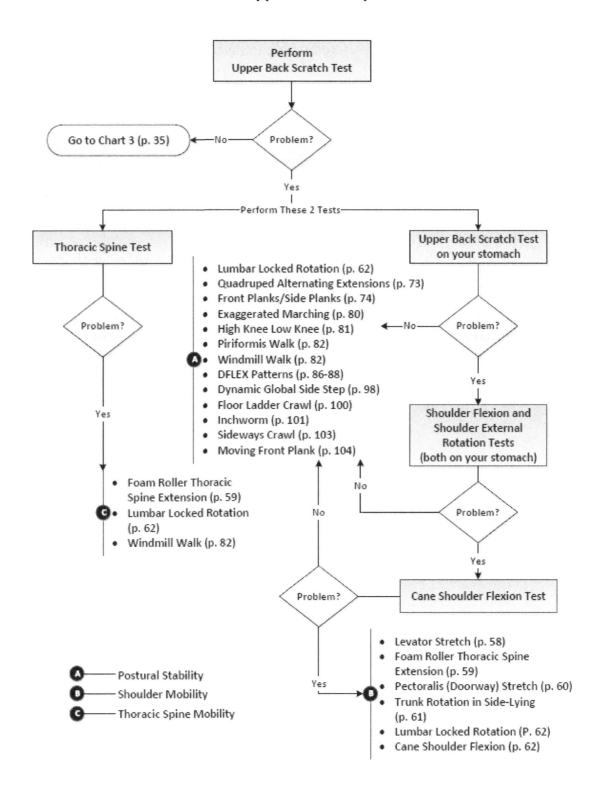

## Quick Reference Sheet 2: Upper Extremity Movement One

Note any trouble spots discovered in your Upper Back Scratch Test assessment by adding a check next to the appropriate test name below. Proceed to the exercises provided in the right column. Record important notes in the space provided below.

| ✔ | Test Name | Category | Exercise Names |
|---|-----------|----------|----------------|
| | Postural Stability | A | Lumbar Locked Rotation (p.62)<br>Quadruped Alternating Extensions (p. 73)<br>Front Planks/Side Planks (p. 74)<br>Exaggerated Marching (p. 80)<br>High Knee Low Knee (p. 81)<br>Piriformis Walk (p. 82)<br>Windmill Walk (p. 82)<br>DFLEX Patterns (pp. 86–88)<br>Dynamic Global Side Step (p. 98)<br>Floor Ladder Crawl (p. 100)<br>Inchworm (p. 101)<br>Sideways Crawl (p. 103)<br>Moving Front Plank (p. 104) |
| | Upper Back Scratch Test on Stomach | B | Levator Stretch (p. 58)<br>Foam Roller Thoracic Spine Extension (p. 59)<br>Pectoralis (Doorway) Stretch (p. 60)<br>Trunk Rotation in Side-Lying (p. 61)<br>Lumbar Locked Rotation (P. 62)<br>Cane Shoulder Flexion (p. 62) |
| | Shoulder Flexion and Shoulder External Rotation Tests (both on stomach) | B | Same as B above |
| | Cane Shoulder Flexion Test | B | Same as B above |
| | Thoracic Spine Test | C | Foam Roller Thoracic Spine Extension (p. 59)<br>Lumbar Locked Rotation (p. 62)<br>Windmill Walk (p. 82) |

Notes: 🐁

_____

_____

_____

_____

## Movement Two: Lower Back Scratch Test

Shoulders have amazing flexibility. If your shoulders are functioning normally, you should be able to reach behind your back from the bottom up. The following movement tests the combination of shoulder extension, shoulder internal rotation, and elbow flexion.

Standing with your feet flat on the floor and close together, reach behind your back as though you are scratching your lower to mid back. Reach your arm up as high as you can in one single, quick action. Do not wriggle your way up! The goal is to see how much you can do without wriggling.

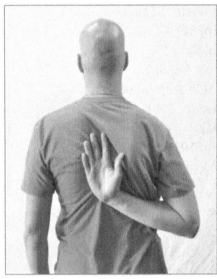

Ch. 2 Fig. 12. Lower Back Scratch

Key points of a normal Lower Back Scratch Test:

- Both hands should be able to reach symmetrical distances.
- Each hand should be able to touch at least the bottom corner, or angle of the shoulder blade on the opposite side.
- The elbow should be flexed completely.
- The shoulder blade should not be sticking out excessively.
- The head should remain in a neutral position (should not jut excessively forward).
- The upper back should not round out.

If you can successfully perform this test, then move on to the Whole Body Extension: Big Overhead Reach section on page 37.

As with the Upper Back Scratch Test on page 25, difficulty with this movement can be broken down into segments to help diagnose the problem. In this case, you want to determine if the problem is tightness in the shoulder, shoulder blade complex, or a postural stability issue.

Postural stability is the first aspect to check as the possible source of your limitation. Do the Lower Back Scratch Test again while lying on your stomach on a table. Try to position yourself so that your neck is as neutral as possible (face down without any rotation). Place your non-test hand under your forehead to keep your neck in a comfortable, neutral position. If you are able to do this movement without any difficulty, your standing posture might have been the problem.

Your fitness program should focus on improving your postural stability utilizing the following exercises.

*Postural Stability Exercises*

Quadruped Alternating Extension p. 73

Windmill Walk p. 82

Upper Body Dynamic Flexibility Patterns pp. 86–88

Ch. 2 Fig. 13. Lower Back Scratch on Table

If you are still unable to perform the Lower Back Scratch Test, proceed to the following Shoulder Complex Tests: Extension and Internal Rotation section. Your goal is to determine whether you have a range of motion, stability, or strength limitation in either shoulder extension or internal rotation.

## Shoulder Complex Tests: Extension and Internal Rotation

To test for a shoulder extension range of motion or strength limitation, lie on your stomach on a table. Lift your arm straight back and up, with your palm facing inward. You should be able to lift your arm about halfway to vertical.

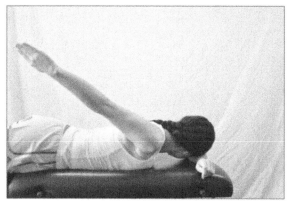

Ch. 2 Fig. 14. Shoulder Extension

If you can perform this test without difficulty, it means you do not have an extension range of motion or strength limitation in the shoulder.

Next, check the internal rotation of your shoulder. Slide over on the table so that your forearm is hanging off but your elbow is supported. While in this position, try to bring your palm parallel to the floor. If you cannot achieve full range of motion, you may have an internal rotation limitation that constricts your ability to reach behind your back effectively. (This motion is described in the Lower Back Scratch Test, beginning on page 32.)

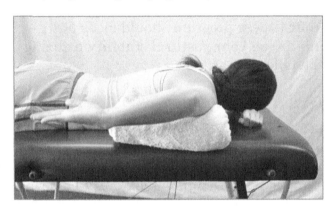

Ch. 2 Fig. 15. Shoulder Internal Rotation

While it may not seem like a big deal, you must be able to reach behind your back to bathe, dress, and perform other everyday tasks. From a physical therapy perspective, limitations in internal rotation also lead to substitutions of other motions that end up straining the shoulder. If you are limited by shoulder extension or internal rotation components of the Lower Back Scratch Test (p. 32), correction exercises are of vital importance. Begin to integrate the following exercises to improve your range of motion and strength in that direction.

*Exercises for Increasing Extension and Internal Rotation*

Cane Shoulder Extension p. 63

Internal Rotation Stretch with Strap p. 63

*Postural Stability Exercises*

Quadruped Alternating Extension p. 73

Front Planks/Side Planks p. 74

Upper Body Dynamic Flexibility Patterns pp. 86–88

**Note**: Limitations in shoulder extension and internal rotation can evolve into complex shoulder problems, regardless of whether they are mobility or stability limitations. If you are experiencing pain with any of these motions or do not make progress with the exercises, consult your healthcare provider.

## Self-Assessment Flow Chart 3: Upper Extremity Movement Two

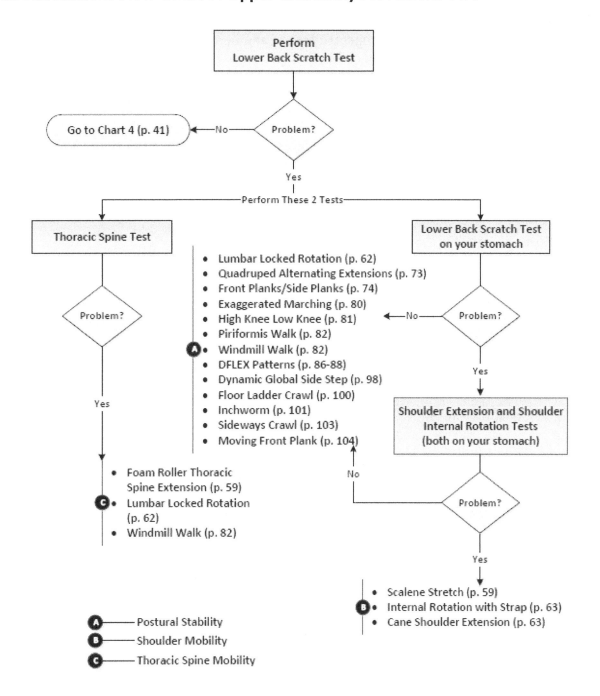

## Quick Reference Sheet 3: Upper Extremity Movement Two

Note any trouble spots discovered in your *Lower Back Scratch Test* assessment by putting a check next to the appropriate test name below. Proceed to the exercises provided in the right column. Record important notes in the space provided below.

| ✔ | Test Name | Category | Exercise Names |
|---|-----------|----------|----------------|
| | Postural Stability | A | Lumbar Locked Rotation (p.62)<br>Quadruped Alternating Extensions (p. 73)<br>Front Planks/Side Planks (p. 74)<br>Exaggerated Marching (p. 80)<br>High Knee Low Knee (p. 81)<br>Piriformis Walk (p. 82)<br>Windmill Walk (p. 82)<br>DFLEX Patterns (pp. 86–88)<br>Dynamic Global Side Step (p. 98)<br>Floor Ladder Crawl (p. 100)<br>Inchworm (p. 101)<br>Sideways Crawl (p. 103)<br>Moving Front Plank (p. 104) |
| | Lower Back Scratch Test on Stomach | B | Scalene Stretch (p. 59)<br>Internal Rotation Stretch with Strap (p. 63)<br>Cane Shoulder Extension (p. 63) |
| | Shoulder Extension and Shoulder Internal Rotation Tests (both on stomach) | B | Same as B above |
| | Thoracic Spine Test | C | Foam Roller Thoracic Spine Extension (p. 59)<br>Lumbar Locked Rotation (p. 62)<br>Windmill Walk (p. 82) |

**Notes:** 📝

_____

_____

_____

_____

_____

_____

_____

_____

## Whole Body Extension: Big Overhead Reach

Being able to extend your whole body is often a difficult motion to perform. In this movement, you are exaggerating the motion of reaching for something overhead.

Stand with your feet flat and together on the floor. Raise your arms up overhead, look up, and reach up and backwards as far as you can. Try to have someone there who can help gauge your range of motion.

Key points of a normal Whole Body Extension: Big Overhead Reach test:

- ✔ The arms should be in line with your ears and core.

- ✔ The spine should curve backward in an evenly rounded fashion. There should not be any pivot points along the spine.

- ✔ The hips should come forward, over, and in front of the toes.

- ✔ The knees should stay fairly straight.

If you are able to perform this motion without any difficulty, move on to the Whole Body Flexion: Forward Bend Test on page 43.

Not being able to do this exercise could indicate range of motion limitations in your spine, shoulders, or hips. If you had difficulty with the movement, you must first check for a range of motion limitation in your thoracic or lumbar spine.

Ch. 2 Fig. 16. Big Overhead Reach

The following Prone Press Up and Thoracic Spine Test: Extension movements will help you detect the problem.

## Prone Press Up

Not unlike the Cobra Pose in yoga, this movement is used to test for range of motion limitations in either the thoracic or lumbar spine.

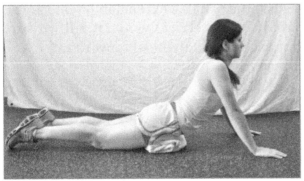

Ch. 2 Fig. 17. Prone Press Up

Begin by lying on your stomach on the floor or a mat. If you don't have someone to observe you, try performing the move in front of a mirror. Place a 2-inch foam pillow or rolled towel under your stomach. With your hands beside your shoulders and elbows at your sides, gently straighten the elbows, pushing your upper body up.

Keep your lower body relaxed on the pillow or towel as you raise the upper body. You should be able to fully straighten your elbows while your hips and pelvis remain on the floor.

If you have an even curve in your lower back, you do not have a limitation in your spine range of motion. If you cannot do the movement, you have a limitation in your lumbar (lower) spine extension.

*Exercises for Increasing Lumbar Extension*

Seated Pelvic Tilting p. 64

Prone On Elbows p. 65

Prone Press Up p. 66

Standing Extensions p. 66

## Thoracic Spine Test: Extension

This thoracic spine extension test is the same movement as the one used to test your thoracic spine rotation. If you found a limitation during the Upper Back Scratch Test on page 25—and performed the Thoracic Spine Test: Rotation on page 28, you do not need to redo this test.

This position tests your ability to fully extend just the thoracic spine. Get down onto your hands and knees into a crawl position on the floor or mat. Your hands are underneath the shoulders and knees under the hips. Now sit back on your heels.

Place your right elbow midline between your knees, but about 2–4 inches in front of them. Bring your left fingertips to your ear. Keeping your butt down against your heels, try to look up toward the ceiling to the left. Repeat on the opposite side.

Ch. 2 Fig. 18. Thoracic Spine Extension

This movement isolates motion to your thoracic spine. This is extension on one side of your thoracic spine. You should be able to rotate symmetrically, about halfway to vertical. If you have a limitation with this exercise, you likely need to work on thoracic spine range of motion and postural strength.

Following are the exercises for thoracic spine range of motion and postural stability.

*Exercises to Increase Thoracic Spine Extension*

Foam Roller Thoracic Spine Extension p. 59

## Hip Extension: Thomas Test

Hip extension is the ability to move your leg back behind your body with the motion coming from your hip. This movement is one of the most common limitations among clients complaining of back, knee, and hip pain regardless of age, sport, or fitness level. The reason? We spend too much time in a flexed position, namely sitting. The widely used Thomas test was developed in the 1800s by British orthopedic surgeon Dr. Hugh Owen Thomas, who used this test to assess muscle tightness of the hip.

When your hip is flexed as in sitting, the muscles in the front get shortened, causing tight hip flexor muscles. Unfortunately, most of us do not take the time to really stretch out our hip flexors. Limited hip extension can cause problems in your back or knees because of compensatory movement patterns that develop in response to tightness. For example, runners with desk jobs often develop tight hip flexors (limited hip extension). When running, the leg must come behind the body on each stride. If the hip can't extend to make that happen, the extension will happen at the lower back, causing an overuse injury in the lower back. The result is back pain when running. Sedentary individuals are even more at risk for biomechanical problems from tight hip flexors.

To test whether you have tight hip flexors, use the Thomas test. Begin by sitting on the very edge of a table or bed. Bring both knees up simultaneously and roll back onto your back. Hold your right knee to your chest as you gently lower your left leg toward the floor. Your knee should lower to below your hip and your back should remain flat. You should also have your knee bent to about 90 degrees or as close as is comfortably possible. If your knee is hanging up in the air higher than your hip, you have tight hip flexors. If your knee does not bend to about 90 degrees or so, you have tight quadriceps muscles. Slowly raise the left leg and bring it toward your chest. Lower the right leg and assess.

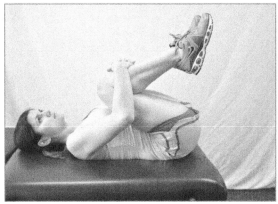

Ch. 2 Fig. 19. Thomas Test

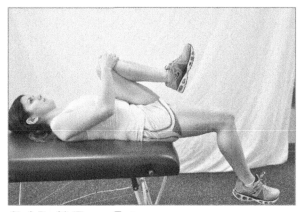

Ch. 2 Fig. 20. Thomas Test

To come out of the test position, bring both knees to your chest, roll to your side, and push up to sitting. *Never sit straight up or dangle both legs off the table at once.* This could injure your lower back.

If you have a history of back problems or feel the position would be too difficult to get into, you can perform this by lying on your back fully on the table, sliding to the side and performing it on one side at a time. *Always keep one knee close to your chest.* Do not release that knee until the other leg is close to your chest. Keeping at least one knee close to your chest prevents your lower back from getting strained.

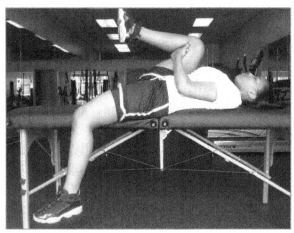

*Exercise for Increasing the Hip Flexor*

Hip Flexor Stretches p. 67–68

Ch. 2. Fig. 21. Thomas Test Modified Position

## Self-Assessment Flow Chart 4: Big Overhead Reach

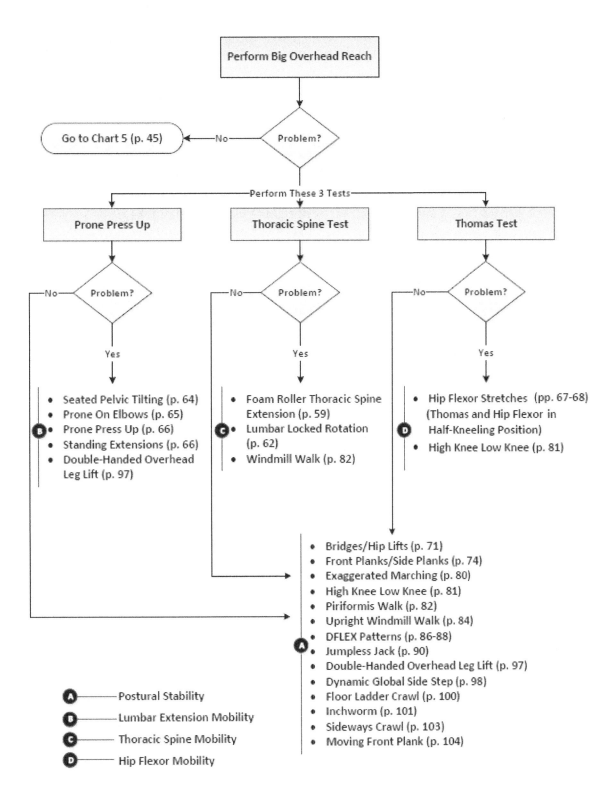

## Quick Reference Sheet 4: Big Overhead Reach

Note any trouble spots discovered in your Big Overhead Reach assessment by putting a check next to the appropriate test name below. Proceed to the exercises provided in the right column. Record important notes in the space provided below.

| ✔ | Test Name | Category | Exercise Names |
|---|---|---|---|
| | Postural Stability | A | Bridges/Hip Lifts (p. 71)<br>Front Planks/Side Planks (p. 74)<br>Exaggerated Marching (p. 80)<br>High Knee Low Knee (p. 81)<br>Piriformis Walk (p. 82)<br>Upright Windmill Walk (p. 84)<br>DFLEX Patterns (pp. 86–88)<br>Jumpless Jack (p. 90)<br>Double-Handed Overhead Leg Lift (p. 97)<br>Dynamic Global Side Step (p. 98)<br>Floor Ladder Crawl (p. 100)<br>Inchworm (p. 101)<br>Sideways Crawl (p. 103)<br>Moving Front Plank (p. 104) |
| | Prone Press Up | B | Seated Pelvic Tilting (p. 64)<br>Prone On Elbows (p. 65)<br>Prone Press Up (p. 66)<br>Standing Extensions (p. 66)<br>Double-Handed Overhead Leg Lift (p. 97) |
| | Thoracic Spine Test | C | Foam Roller Thoracic Spine Extension (p. 59)<br>Lumbar Locked Rotation (p. 62)<br>Windmill Walk (p. 82) |
| | Thomas Test | D | Hip Flexor Stretches (pp. 67-68) (Thomas and Hip Flexor in Half-Kneeling Position)<br>High Knee Low Knee (p. 81) |

**Notes:**

## Whole Body Flexion: Forward Bend Test

Forward flexion is the ability to bend forward. When you get out of a chair or pick things up off the floor, you are performing the familiar motion called forward flexion.

Ch. 2 Fig. 22. Forward Bend

Standing with your feet flat and together, bend forward as if you are trying to touch your toes. Keep your knees straight. If you are able to perform this movement without any difficulty, proceed to the Deep Squat section on page 47.

Key points of a normal Whole Body Flexion: Forward Bend Test:

- ✔ Your back should have a smooth even curve.
- ✔ Your knees should be straight.
- ✔ You should be able to touch your toes.

Limitations with forward flexion can come from tightness in your spine, hips, or hamstrings. To further assess the limitation, complete the following Child's Pose and Straight Leg Raise/Hamstring Test sections.

## Child's Pose

If you are a yoga aficionado, you will be comfortable performing the exercise known as Child's Pose. I use this movement as a way to test whether you have full range of motion in your hips and spine.

Start by getting onto your hands and knees. Sit your buttocks back onto your heels with your arms outstretched. If you cannot get your heels to your butt and feel strain in your hips and lower back, you likely have hip and spine mobility limitation. If your lower back does not round out in this position, you likely have a lumbar spine range of motion limitation.

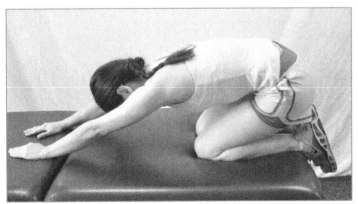

Ch. 2 Fig. 23. Child's Pose on Table

An alternate position you can use to test hip motion is to lie on your back and bring your knees up toward your chest. This motion will completely bend your hips. If you feel that your midsection is limiting you, position your legs to the side slightly while bringing your knees up toward your chest. This small modification will still allow you to obtain a valid hip mobility assessment. Whether you use the modification or not, you should be able to bring your knees very close to your chest, evenly on both sides. If you can't do so, there is likely a limitation with your hip flexibility.

Key points of a normal Child's Pose:

✓ You should be able to touch your stomach to your thighs without stressing your hips and lower back.

*Exercises for Increasing Hip, Knee, and Lumbar Mobility*

Child's Pose (the test becomes the exercise)

Seated Forward Flexion Stretch p. 64

Roll Up Series p. 104

## Straight Leg Raise/Hamstring Test

If you suspect tight hamstrings, the best way to assess them is to perform a straight leg raise test. Lying on your back and keeping your knee straight, lift your right leg up toward the ceiling. You should be able to lift your leg to vertical. If it feels difficult to raise the leg because of a weakness, you can use a strap to assist you. (For a picture of this exercise using a strap, see the Hamstring Stretch on page 69 of this book.) Now do the same movement using your left leg. If you cannot achieve a near vertical orientation of either leg, you likely have hamstring tightness. The following exercises will help you with hamstring tightness.

Ch. 2 Fig. 24. Straight Leg Raise/Hamstring

*Exercises for Increasing Hamstring Length*

Hamstring Stretch p. 69

Windmill Walk p. 82

Upright Windmill Walk p. 84

Bobbing Bird p. 91

Inchworm p. 101

Double-Handed Overhead Leg Lift p. 97

## Self-Assessment Flow Chart 5: Forward Bend Test

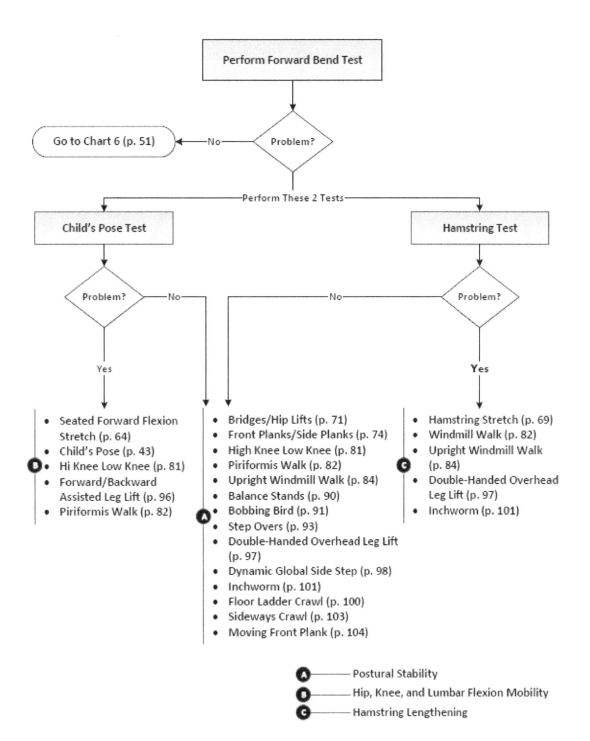

## Quick Reference Sheet 5: Forward Bend Test

Note any trouble spots discovered in your Forward Bend Test by putting a check next to the appropriate test name below. Proceed to the exercises provided in the right column. Record important notes in the space provided below.

| ✔ | Test Name | Category | Exercise Names |
|---|-----------|----------|----------------|
| | Postural Stability | A | Bridges/Hip Lifts (p. 71)<br>Front Planks/Side Planks (p. 74)<br>High Knee Low Knee (p. 81)<br>Piriformis Walk (p. 82)<br>Upright Windmill Walk (p. 84)<br>Balance Stands (p. 90)<br>Bobbing Bird (p. 91)<br>Step Overs (p. 93)<br>Double-Handed Overhead Leg Lift (p. 97)<br>Dynamic Global Side Step (p. 98)<br>Floor Ladder Crawl (p. 100)<br>Inchworm (p. 101)<br>Sideways Crawl (p. 103)<br>Moving Front Plank (p. 104) |
| | Child's Pose | B | Child's Pose (p. 43)<br>Seated Forward Flexion Stretch (p. 64)<br>High Knee Low Knee (p. 81)<br>Piriformis Walk (p. 82)<br>Forward/Backward Assisted Leg Lift (p. 96) |
| | Hamstring | C | Hamstring Stretch (p. 69)<br>Windmill Walk (p. 82)<br>Upright Windmill Walk (p. 84)<br>Inchworm (p. 101) |

**Notes:** ✍

_____

_____

_____

_____

_____

_____

_____

## Deep Squat

The single most functional activity that few want to do but is of vital importance is the deep squat. There is really no way around it! What *is* a proper functional squat? Minimally, your thighs need to be parallel to the floor because that is the height of most chairs and toilets. You should not need an external prop to use one. Ideally, you should be able to lower your hips below the horizontal plane of your knees, which is a full or deep squat.

Begin by standing with your feet slightly wider than shoulder-width apart.

Keep your toes pointed forward throughout the squat. Raise your arms overhead.

To help keep your shoulders in proper alignment, hold a stick or broom. Push your butt back and lower it toward the floor.

Ch. 2 Fig. 25. Deep Squat with Stick

Key points of a normal Deep Squat:

- ✔ Your toes should remain pointed forward throughout the movement.
- ✔ Your heels should remain in contact with the floor throughout the movement.
- ✔ Your knees should not come in front of your toes and should stay in line with your toes.
- ✔ Your core area should be straight with a smooth spine.
- ✔ Your core and your lower legs should be parallel.
- ✔ Your eyes should be looking straight ahead so as to keep your head and neck in a neutral position.
- ✔ Your arms should be straight and in line with your ears.
- ✔ Your butt should lower so that your thighs are at minimum parallel to the floor, if not deeper.

Ch. 2 Fig. 26. Deep Squat Side View

If you are able to perform this squat without difficulty, move on to the Single Limb Balance Test on page 50. If you had difficulty with this test, do the exercises in the Ankle Mobility Test and Strength Limitations sections.

## Ankle Mobility Test

If you are unable to squat properly, check first for a possible limitation of the ankle joint. If your ankle is functioning normally, you will be able to flex your toes in an upward direction to 20 degrees. This motion is called dorsiflexion.

Ch. 2 Fig. 27. Limited Squat Mechanics

Ch. 2 Fig. 28. Improved Squat Mechanics

In figure 27, this client demonstrates tight ankles that are limiting the ability to squat properly. Using the Ankle Mobility Test to remove ankle motion from the squat, figure 28 shows the client's improved squat mechanics. The client's limited squat function is being caused by an ankle mobility limitation.

There are two ways to test for ankle joint mobility problems.

1.  Place a block or 2–3 inch board under your heels and try the deep squat again. If you are now able to squat without difficulty, it means that you have an ankle limitation.

    If you had difficulty with this first test, perform the second test on the next page. There is still the question of whether the limitation is calf muscle tightness or with the ankle joint itself.

2. Put your foot on a chair and lunge forward, bringing your knee over your toes. If you cannot bring your knee over your toes by about 5 inches, it means there is a limitation in your ankle joint mobility.

Ch. 2 Fig. 29. Ankle Mobility Test 2

If you are able to do the second test with ease but not the first ankle test, it means that you have calf muscle tightness.

*Exercises for Increasing Ankle and Calf Mobility*

Calf Stretch p. 69

Ankle Dorsiflexion Mobility p. 70

## Hip, Knee, and Lumbar Mobility

In the Whole Body Flexion: Forward Bend Test section, you learned how to test for tightness in the lumbar spine and hamstrings. Tightness in any of these areas also makes it difficult for you to perform the Deep Squat. If you have not already done so, return to page 43 to check your hip, knee, and lumbar flexion.

## Strength Limitations

Squatting takes a fair amount of strength throughout your core area, hips, and legs. Squatting is an excellent way to identify strength limitations in these areas. If you are not able keep your knee in line with your toes and they tend to come closer together, you likely have weakness in your hip muscles. If you tend to pitch your core forward but do not have any range of motion limitations, you likely have a weakness in your core or hip extensors. Quad weakness is often demonstrated as the inability to lower your butt below parallel to the floor. All of these aberrant movements in the absence of range of motion limitations indicate a weakness. The following exercises are specifically designed to strengthen muscles that impact functional squatting.

*Exercises for Improving Hip Abductor Strength*

## Single Limb Balance

As discussed in Chapter 1, balance is a critical component of the body's normal functional movement.

Being able to balance on one leg is necessary for negotiating obstacles as we walk. Without being able to do so, even for a short period of time, we would be at great risk for falling. Ten seconds is considered the normal amount of time one should be able to stand on one foot.

To perform this test, stand on a flat surface and lift your right knee toward your chest so that your femur is at least parallel to the floor or a bit higher.

With your arms at your sides, balance for 10 seconds. Now do the same test using your left knee. The Single Limb Balance stance tests your hip strength and stability as well as your balance system.

Note that we often overuse vision and underutilize the other two systems to help us balance. For example: if you close your eyes and perform the same single limb balance test, you will find that you wobble much more. If you are unable to hold the position with your eyes closed, you are probably relying heavily on your visual system. All dynamic flexibility exercises will help you improve your balance system.

Ch. 2 Fig. 30. Single Limb Balance

# Self-Assessment Flow Chart 6: Squat Test

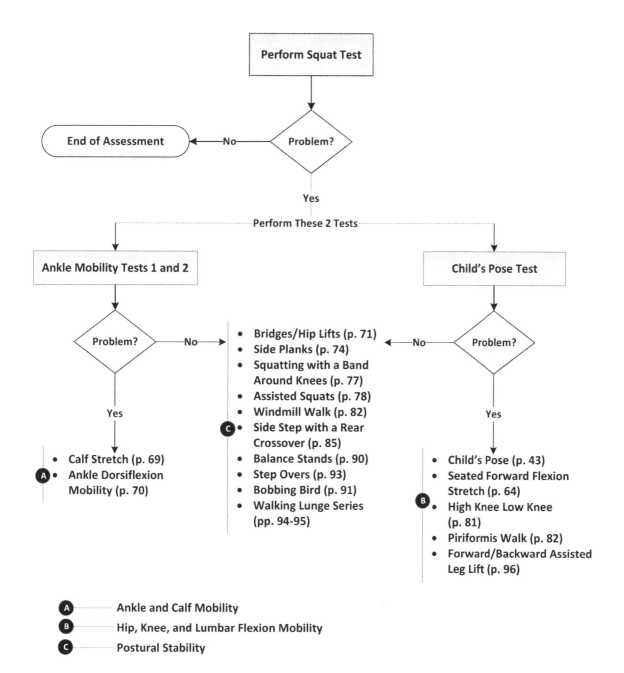

## Quick Reference Sheet 6: Squat Test

Note any trouble spots discovered in your Squat Test by putting a check next to the appropriate test name below. Proceed to the exercises provided in the right column. Record important notes in the space provided below.

| ✔ | Test Name | Category | Exercise Names |
|---|---|---|---|
| | Ankle Mobility Tests 1 and 2 | A | Calf Stretch (p. 69)<br>Ankle Dorsiflexion Mobility (p. 70) |
| | Child's Pose Test | B | Child's Pose (p. 43)<br>Seated Forward Flexion Stretch (p. 64)<br>High Knee Low Knee (p. 81)<br>Piriformis Walk (p. 82)<br>Forward/Backward Assisted Leg Lift (p. 96) |
| | Postural Stability | C | Bridges/Hip Lifts (p. 71)<br>Side Planks (p. 74)<br>Squatting with a Band Around Knees (p. 77)<br>Assisted Squats (p. 78)<br>Windmill Walk (p. 82)<br>Side Step with a Rear Crossover (p. 85)<br>Balance Stands (p. 90)<br>Bobbing Bird (p. 91)<br>Step Overs (p. 93)<br>Walking Lunge Series (pp. 94–95) |

Notes: 🖎

_____

_____

_____

_____

_____

_____

_____

_____

_____

# Summary

Congratulations on completing your functional movement self-assessment. These movements transcend age categories and functional levels. We all have to get dressed, bend forward, reach overhead, and get off a seat, no matter what our age or fitness level.

This assessment was designed and sequenced to help you discover possible challenges or limitations to your foundational fitness. It is not a comprehensive examination, but it *is* an essential tool to help you be more in tune with your body and its abilities. Once you find your strengths and limitations, you can use this awareness to build a more intelligent and purposeful fitness plan. Keep in mind that we tend to naturally move in the path of least resistance. It is imperative that you maintain a proactive approach to working on your challenges in order to build foundational fitness.

If you find any of these movements to be painful, you should seek the advice of your healthcare professional.

# Chapter 3: Building Your Foundation

## ❧ Be Fit First. ☙

The results of your functional movement self-assessment may or may not have surprised you. Were you awesome—with near perfect flexibility, balance, and full functional movement of not just your individual joints but whole body? If so, consider yourself blessed.

As is more likely the case, many of us have one or more limitations with aspects of our physical movement, balance, strength, stability, and neurological control. As you learned in Chapter 1, dynamic flexibility is an intricate juxtaposition of these components. My clients—including elite athletes—almost always work with one, several, or quite a few of these specific rehabilitative exercises. Whether rehabilitating an old football injury, working on posture, or developing strength to take on those planks, use these exercises to address any limitations.

**Note**: The exercises in Chapters 3–4 can be performed with or without shoes, depending on your comfort level and the cleanliness of your environment.

### Chin Tuck

The Chin Tuck is a misunderstood and often improperly utilized exercise. The goal of the Chin Tuck is to create cervical retraction. Cervical retraction is the ability of the cervical spine to stack the vertebrae on top of each other like a column. Most of us spend our time in the opposite position of retraction, called protraction.

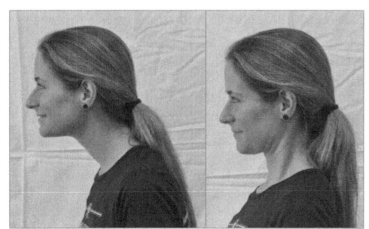

Ch. 3 Fig. 1. Protraction (Forward) and Retraction (Backward)

When you are in a protracted position for long periods of time, there is a lot of increased pressure and stress on the structures around the neck. This includes the neck muscles and joints. The Chin Tuck can help you work on improving your head position and posture, as well as reducing the muscle strain in your neck. You can do this exercise lying down, seated, or standing. You should take your time to master the Chin Tuck in a lying position before moving to the seated and standing positions. You may feel confident enough to progress within one session, or you may need weeks of practice.

Lie on your back on the floor or mat. Imagine an invisible rod passing through your ears to stabilize your head as you gently nod it down slightly. Keep your head on the floor or mat with your shoulders gently pressed back and your back flat, gazing directly toward the ceiling. Gently push your head backwards onto the mat as if you are trying to flatten your neck out. This is not an aggressive technique, but a gentle movement to help correct posture and strengthen the small muscles that help hold the head properly.

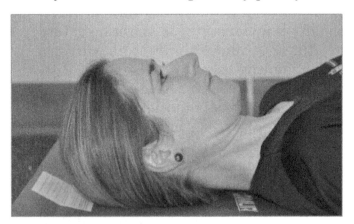

Return to your starting position and repeat 1–30 times.

Ch. 3 Fig. 2. Chin Tuck on Mat

In the seated position, make sure you are sitting supported and with good posture. Keep your gaze straight ahead as you gently tilt your chin downward and pull your head back. This movement reminds us of a pigeon that bobs its head forward and backward as it walks. This can be challenging to achieve and sometimes requires several weeks of practice to get it right. Do not push excessively. This, like all the movements in the book, may be difficult to do. The Chin Tuck may also be slightly uncomfortable, but it should be absolutely pain free. Once you have mastered the seated position, you can begin to implement the Chin Tuck standing any time you feel you need to improve your posture. Repeat 1–30 times.

## Chin Tuck and Rotate

The Chin Tuck and Rotate should also initially be performed while lying down before you progress to a sitting or standing position.

While lying, nod your head so that your chin lowers slightly but your head remains on the floor or mat. Keep your gaze directly toward the ceiling. Instead of pushing your head into the mat and flattening your neck, maintain the Chin Tuck while you turn your head to the right. Turn gently as far as you can. Return to your starting position and rotate to the left, looking in the direction you want your head to move. Vision is a powerful assistant to these rotational neck movements! Repeat 1–30 times.

Over time, progress this exercise to a sitting position. Make sure you are sitting with good posture. Keep your gaze straight ahead as you gently tilt your chin downward and rotate your neck to the right. Come back to your starting position, perform another Chin Tuck, and turn to the left. Once you have mastered the sitting position, progress toward standing. Repeat 1–20 times.

Ch. 3 Fig. 3. Chin Tuck

Ch. 3 Fig. 4. Chin Tuck and Rotate

## Chin Tuck and Extend

Limitations in neck extension are very common. Being able to look up is important in daily life, but we seldom take time to work on it. Neck extension exercises can improve your ability to look up and also help correct posture when done correctly.

This exercise is best performed while seated. In a sitting position with good posture, keep your gaze straight ahead as you gently tilt your chin downward. Slowly and gently look up toward the ceiling, moving one vertebra at a time from the head to the base of the neck. Return to your starting position.

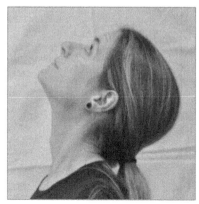

At first, the Chin Tuck and Extend will be difficult to perform but will get easier with practice. If you have any known conditions that may affect your blood pressure or if you have vertigo, use extra caution with this movement. If you experience dizziness, nausea, or pain at any time, stop immediately and consult your healthcare provider.

Repeat 1–20 times.

Ch. 3 Fig. 5. Chin Tuck and Extend

## Chin Tuck and Roll

Limitations in neck flexion can be addressed by
performing a Chin Tuck and Roll.

Bring your chin toward your chest as if you were
rolling down one vertebra at a time. The goal of this
movement is to feel a stretch in the neck from the base
of your skull down to the upper back. As you come
back up, reverse the process by moving one vertebra at
a time from the upper back to the base of the skull.

Repeat 1–20 times.

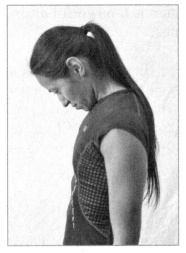

Ch. 3 Fig. 6. Chin Tuck and Roll

## Levator Stretch

The levator scapula is a muscle that originates in your upper neck and ends at the
top corner of the shoulder blade. This is the muscle people complain about when
there are tight *knots* in the neck and shoulders. Because of forward head posture,
the levator scapulae often overwork by having to hold the head up most of the day.
If you have good posture, the head is well balanced on top of the neck. A
well-balanced neck is much like a golf ball that sits perfectly on top of its tee. A
head balanced on top of the neck reduces the strain on the neck muscles.

In a sitting or standing position, bring your right hand up and over your head and
reach for your left shoulder blade. Be careful not to let your arm push your head
forward or downward. You should be able to look straight ahead with your head in a
comfortable, neutral position.

With your neck in this position, gently rotate to the left as far as possible. Now look
down toward your left armpit and bring your chin down until you feel a stretch in
the lower neck region on the right. You should perform this stretch for at least 30
seconds at a time. Repeat 2–3 times on each side.

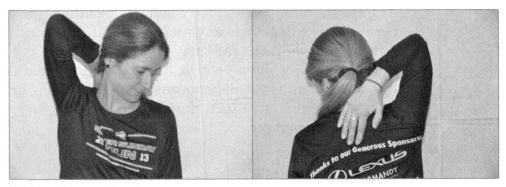

Ch. 3 Fig. 7. Levator Stretch

## Scalene Stretch

The scalene muscles are located in the front of the neck. They can often get tightened, and shorten when you have poor posture. As with the cervical extension exercises, use caution when performing this stretch. If you feel pain, dizziness, or lightheadedness, stop and consult your healthcare provider. Otherwise, the Scalene Stretch is an excellent way to increase mobility in the neck. This exercise is best performed while sitting or standing.

In the sitting or standing position with good posture, tilt your head toward the left so that the left ear moves toward the left shoulder. *Do not elevate the left shoulder!* It may help to grasp your right wrist (that is behind your back) with your left hand, creating a wing on the left. Once your head is tilted to a stretched position, begin to look up toward the ceiling. You may rotate your head to the left or right to change the stretch slightly. Where you feel the most stretch is most likely *what* you need to stretch the most. Repeat the stretch on the opposite side.

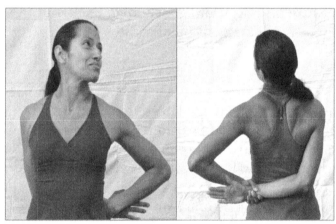

Ch. 3 Fig. 8. Scalene Stretch

Hold for 30 seconds 2–3 times on each side.

## Foam Roller Thoracic Spine Extension

The thoracic spine refers to your upper back. In its normal state, the thoracic spine has a natural curve to it. However, people tend to spend too much time in a slouched position often characterized by improper forward head posture. This Foam Roller Thoracic Spine Extension is used to create more extension in the thoracic spine. If a foam roller is too firm, you can start with something softer, such as a pillow.

Begin by sitting on the floor or bed—preferably one with a firm surface. Place the pillow or roller just below your shoulder blades. Carefully lean back over the pillow or roller, keeping your hands behind your head to support the neck and head. There should never be any strain on your head or neck.

To get the most out of the stretch, you may have to move the pillow or roller up or down a bit.

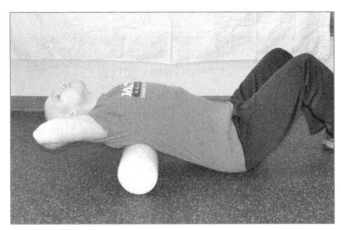

Ch. 3 Fig. 9. Thoracic Spine Extension

Depending on your tolerance for the pressure and position, gently rock back and forth on a tight spot or knot 1–30 times. Or, hold the position of stretch for 30 seconds 2–3 times.

## Pectoralis (Doorway) Stretch

The pectoralis muscles are located in the front of the chest. These muscles can shorten easily when we spend a lot of time in a slouched position. Stretching out the pectoralis muscles can help you improve your posture. There are many ways to stretch the pectoralis muscles. Start with the following simple doorway stretch.

Ch. 3 Fig. 10. Pectoralis Stretch
Front View

Stand in a doorway and place one arm on each side of the door frame. Start with your shoulders and elbows bent to about 90 degrees.

Now step forward with one foot and shift your weight onto the foot until you feel a stretch across your chest. There should be no strain in your shoulders. The height of your arm placement is what will determine where you feel the stretch. If you place your arms higher, you will feel the stretch lower in your chest and vice versa.

Hold the stretch for 30 seconds and repeat 2–3 times.

Ch. 3 Fig. 11. Pectoralis Stretch Side View

## Trunk Rotation in Side-Lying

If you performed the thoracic spine rotation test as part of your self-assessment and discovered you have limitations, you'll find this exercise very useful. Trunk Rotation in Side-Lying can help increase your range of motion (ROM) into both extension and rotation.

Start by lying on your right side on the floor or mat. Bring your knees up toward your chest so that your hips and knees are bent to about 90 degrees. Place your right hand on your knees to help keep them in position. Gently twist your body to the left, creating left rotation in your spine. You can intensify this stretch by reaching to the left with your left arm.

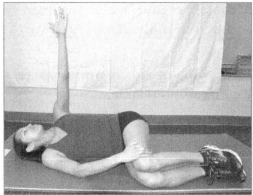
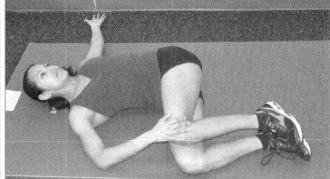

Ch. 3 Fig. 12. Trunk Rotation in Side-Lying      Ch. 3 Fig. 13. Trunk Rotation with Intensified Stretch

Hold this position for 30 seconds and repeat 2–3 times on each side.

## Lumbar Locked Rotation

The thoracic spine rotation test in the self-assessment on page 28 (Thoracic Spine Test: Rotation) and the Lumbar Locked Rotation movements are the same. This exercise is designed to help you increase range of motion and strengthen your thoracic spine muscles.

Ch. 3 Fig. 14. Lumbar Locked Rotation

Start on your hands and knees. Bend your knees and sit back on your heels as far as you comfortably can. Position your right elbow between both knees and place the elbow about 2–4 inches in *front* of them on the table or mat. Take your left hand and place your fingers by your ears or on your upper back. Keep your head in good alignment with your body. Resist the temptation to let your head bend forward during the movement. Turn your head and trunk to the left as though you are trying to look up at the ceiling.

To achieve the maximum benefit of this exercise, squeeze your left shoulder blade toward your spine.

Repeat 1–30 times on each side.

## Cane Shoulder Flexion

If you have shoulder flexion range of motion limitations, you can work on your flexibility using the Cane Shoulder Flexion.

Begin by lying on your back, holding a cane or dowel in both hands. For best results, lie on a flat, firm surface. Make sure you have a lot of room to bring your arms overhead. With your hands about shoulder-width apart, bring your hands and the cane overhead and toward the floor. Let your arms stretch as far back as they can go. As you stretch, be sure to keep your ribs and back on the table. Avoid arching to compensate for decreased shoulder motion.

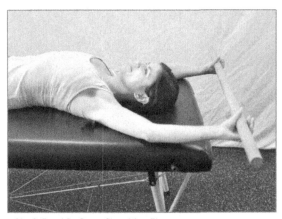

Ch. 3 Fig. 15. Cane Shoulder Flexion

Repeat this movement slowly and in a controlled manner 1–30 times.

## Cane Shoulder Extension

If you have trouble reaching behind your back because of a shoulder extension limitation, use this Cane Shoulder Extension exercise.

In a standing position, place a cane or rod behind your back. With your palms facing the wall, lift the cane away from your body while keeping your back and neck in a neutral and upright position.

Repeat 1–30 times.

Ch. 3 Fig. 16. Cane Shoulder Extension

## Internal Rotation Stretch with Strap

This exercise is designed to help you improve your flexibility with internal rotation, or reaching behind your back.

While standing, place a strap (a belt or towel will also work) over your left shoulder. Reach behind your back with your right hand and grasp the strap. Gently use the strength of your left hand to pull the right hand up your back until you feel a stretch. You may find this position uncomfortable. Make sure you have good posture and go *slowly* into the stretch.

Hold for 10–30 seconds 3–5 times on each side.

When you come out of the stretch, it is not uncommon to feel a bit stiff in the shoulder. To alleviate any residual stiffness, follow up with the Cane Shoulder Flexion exercise on page 62.

Ch. 3 Fig. 17. Internal Rotation Stretch with Strap

## Seated Pelvic Tilting

Seated Pelvic Tilting is an excellent exercise for increasing mobility in both the flexion and extension of your lower back. Begin seated on a chair or exercise ball. Gently round your lower back out, as though you were slouching.

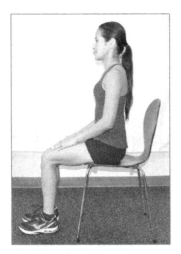

Ch. 3 Fig. 18. Seated Pelvic Tilting (Starting Position)

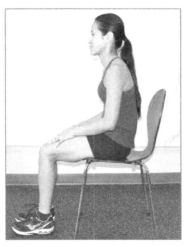

Ch. 3 Fig. 19. Seated Pelvic Tilting (Slouch Position)

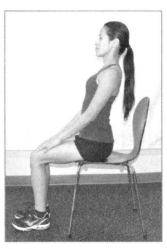

Ch. 3 Fig. 20. Seated Pelvic Tilting (Arch Position)

Now tilt your pelvis forward; you are arching your lower back so that your tailbone lifts off the seat and your stomach sticks out in front. Repeat tilting forward and backward to loosen your lower back. When done, come to a resting position in which your pelvis is neutral. Repeat 1–30 times.

**Tip**: When tilting, picture a bowl with water in it. The bowl is your pelvis. When you are slouched, water will pour out the back of the bowl. When you arch, water will pour out the front of the bowl.

## Seated Forward Flexion Stretch

If you found that you had difficulty bending forward during the self-assessment because of a range of motion limitation, try this Seated Forward Flexion Stretch.

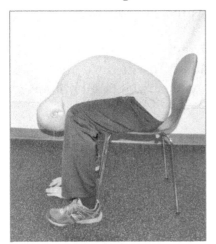

Ch. 3 Fig. 21. Seated Forward Flexion Stretch

Begin in a sitting position. Bring your knees and feet apart. Bend forward and reach to the floor. Bend as far forward as you comfortably can until you feel a stretch in your lower back. Using your hands, come back up slowly to return to the sitting position.

Hold 2–30 seconds 1–10 times.

## Lumbar Extensions

There are multiple ways to work on increasing lumbar extension mobility. The simplest way is the Seated Pelvic Tilting exercise on p. 64. To increase the intensity of your extension exercises, progress through the following: Prone On Elbows, Prone Press Up, and Standing Extensions.

## Prone On Elbows

Lie with your hips on the floor or mat with a 2-inch foam pillow or rolled towel under your stomach for comfort. Allow your butt and lower back to relax as you keep your hips on the floor.

**Tip**: To help relax the butt and lower back, try turning your toes inward.

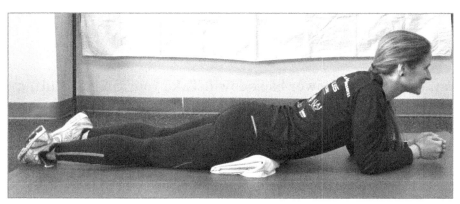

Ch. 3 Fig. 22. Prone On Elbows Starting Position

Now push up through your shoulder blades to keep your head up and looking straight ahead.

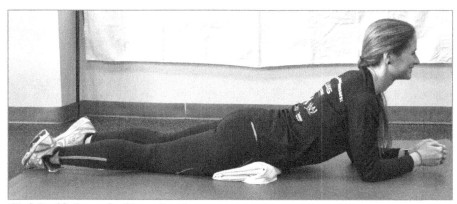

Ch. 3 Fig. 23. Prone On Elbows Position

Raise and lower 1–20 times as tolerated.

## Prone Press Up

The Prone Press Up is an advanced version of the lumbar extension. This is the same movement you performed during the self-assessment.

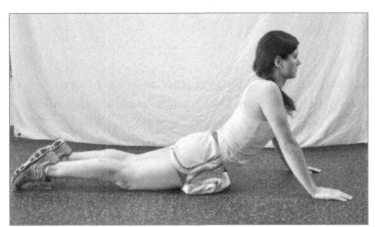

Lie with your hips on the floor or mat with a 2-inch foam pillow or rolled towel under your stomach. Place your hands by your shoulders. Press up by straightening your elbows.

*Keep your lower back relaxed!*

Ch. 3. Fig. 24. Prone Press Up

Push up as far as you can tolerate then lower back down. Take your time executing the movement. Repeat 1–20 times as tolerated.

## Standing Extensions

You can also perform a lumbar extension in the standing position. For most people, the standing extension is a much more convenient position.

Begin in a standing position with your feet a little wider than hip width. Place your hands on your waist so that your thumbs rest comfortably on your lower back and your first finger rests on your pelvis. Keep your gaze straight ahead; do not look up at the ceiling. Lean back from the waist to create an arch in your lower back.

Repeat 1–20 times.

Ch. 3. Fig. 25. Standing Extension

## Hip Flexor Stretches

Tight hip flexors are associated with back, knee, and hip problems. In our culture of sitting, hip flexors often get neglected.

This section contains the Thomas Test from the self-assessment, as well as its modified version in case you have back issues or difficulty concerns. The Thomas Test is an excellent way to stretch the hip flexors. We've also included an effective alternative to the Thomas Test, a hip flexor stretch in the half-kneeling position.

In the Thomas Test, begin by sitting on the very edge of a table or bed. Roll back as you bring both knees up to your chest. Still holding your right knee to your chest, gently lower your left leg toward the floor. Allow the lowered left leg to fully relax. Once the lowered leg feels thoroughly relaxed, slowly bring both knees *back* to your chest. Switch sides by lowering your right leg while still holding your left knee to your chest. Allow the lowered right leg to fully relax and then return to your starting position.

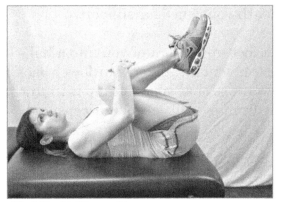
Ch. 3 Fig. 26. Thomas Test

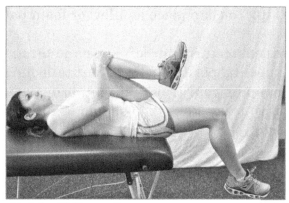
Ch. 3 Fig. 27. Thomas Test

To avoid injury or strain to your lower back:
- *Always* bring both legs back up to your chest first before relaxing the opposite side.
- *Always* keep one knee close to your chest at all times.
- *Never* release one knee until the other leg is close to your chest.
- *Never* sit up straight or dangle both legs off the table at once.
- *Always* bring both knees to your chest, roll to your side, and push up to sitting to come out of the position.

Hold for 30 seconds 2–3 times on each side.

If you have a history of back problems or feel the position is too difficult, you can perform this by lying on your back fully on the table, sliding to the side and performing it on one side at a time. Always keep one knee close to your chest.

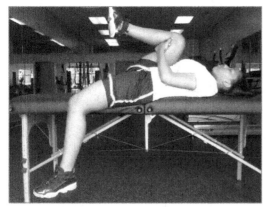

Do not release that knee until the other leg is close to your chest. Keeping at least one knee close to your chest prevents your lower back from getting strained.

Ch. 3 Fig. 28. Thomas Test Modified Position

The following hip flexor stretch is an option to the Thomas Test and is performed in the half-kneeling position on the floor.

**Tip**: You can place a pillow or foam pad underneath your knee for support.

Kneel on just your left knee and bring your right foot up in front of you into a half-kneeling position. (Tuck your tailbone slightly to prevent strain on your lower back.) Keeping your trunk upright, bring your hips forward so that your left hip is in *front* of your left knee. You should feel a stretch in the front of your left quadriceps and into your hip.

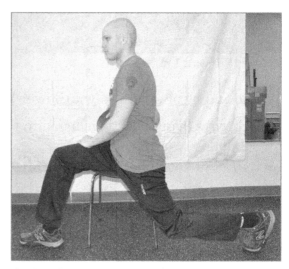

Ch. 3 Fig. 29. Hip Flexor in Half-Kneeling Position      Ch. 3 Fig. 30. Hip Flexor Modified Position with Chair

Hold for 30 seconds 2–3 times on each side.

**Tip**: If kneeling is difficult or hard on your knees, you can use a chair.

## Hamstring Stretch

The following Hamstring Stretch is just one of several methods used to stretch the hamstrings. This method is great because it protects the lower back from excessive strain. If you have back issues, we highly recommend this stretch.

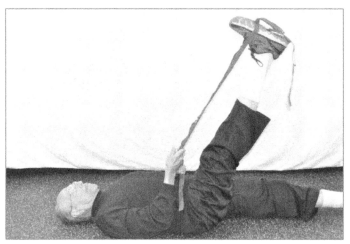

Ch. 3 Fig. 31. Hamstring Stretch with Strap

Lie on your back on the floor or mat. Place a strap or belt around your right foot. A yoga or exercise strap is ideal.

Lift the right foot up, using your arms and strap to pull the leg up high enough to create a stretch on the back of the leg. Be sure to keep your knee straight. Hold the position for 30 seconds 2–3 times on each leg.

## Calf Stretch

The calf muscle crosses both the ankle joint and the knee joint. It is imperative to keep the calf muscle limber to promote good functional mechanics when squatting or bending backward.

For this Calf Stretch exercise, you'll need a half foam roller or a book about 2–3 inches thick. Place the ball of your foot on the roller or book, keeping your heel *down* on the floor. Stand up straight and tall and think about bringing your hips over your toes. Hold for 30 seconds 2–3 times on each calf.

Ch. 3 Fig. 32. Calf Stretch

### Ankle Dorsiflexion Mobility

Another method of increasing ankle mobility is a modified lunge on the floor or a chair. With one foot in a half-kneeling position on the floor or a chair, try to bring your knee as far in front of your toes as you can. This is the same movement as the Ankle Mobility Test 2 described in the self-assessment, beginning on p. 48.

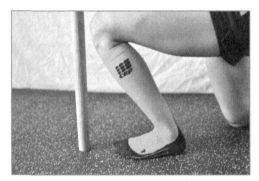

Ch. 3 Fig. 33. Modified Lunge on Floor

Ch. 3 Fig. 34. Modified Lunge on Chair

Repeat 1–30 times on each side slowly and deliberately.

# Full Body Strengthening

The exercises in this section are designed to help you develop full body strength. To help avoid the risk of injury, I work with and—after nearly 20 years—continue to recommend the 10% rule. This rule describes the principle of gradual adaptation to exercise. Your body needs time to adjust to an increased training work load, which can be measured by quantity, intensity, or time. In running, for example, the rule is that one's weekly mileage should never increase more than 10% over the previous week.[1] In triathlon, USA Triathlon coaches learn to use the 10% rule for running, cycling, *and* swimming, which is a low impact sport.[2] Depending on the multisport training phase or plan, the 10% rule can be applied on a daily, weekly, or monthly basis.

When building your foundational fitness with these exercises, do not increase repetitions or time by more than 10% from one session to the next. In fact, clients are often encouraged to begin with a smaller percentage until they master an exercise with good form. If you are a beginning exerciser, the 10% rule can be your 3% rule. Or 5%. Whether you are a novice or skilled athlete, begin conservatively and build gradually to reduce your risk of injury.

---

[1] Amby Burfoot, "The 10-Percent Rule," *Runners World*, November 14, 2001, accessed June 11, 2019, http://www.runnersworld.com/running-tips /the-10-percent-rule.

[2] Sara McLarty, and Misty Becerra, "Swimming Technique and Training," in *USA Triathlon Level 1 Coaching Certification Manual*, (Colorado Springs: USA Triathlon, 2011), 23.

**Guidelines for Strengthening Safely**

Use the following guidelines to help you build your strength safely.

1. Select your training measure. You can choose repetitions or time, which is also an excellent measure. 30 repetitions are equal to approximately one minute. People often use both measures within a workout, depending on the exercise. For a static exercise such as a front plank, time is an excellent measure. For a dynamic exercise such as a quadruped alternating extension, repetition is an excellent measure. Choose the measure or combination of measures that work best for you.

2. Follow the 10% (or less) rule when increasing the quantity, intensity, or time you spend from one session to the next. For example: if you perform 10 repetitions of an exercise with good form, you can attempt 11 repetitions of the exercise in your next session. If you can hold a plank for one minute using good form, try to hold it for a minute and six seconds the next time. Make adjustments to this rule as needed to achieve your best and safest results.

3. Master each exercise in the sequence provided before you increase your training work load! This progression is purposeful and will help you safely adapt from a basic to a more advanced level.

**Bridges/Hip Lifts**

The Bridges/Hip Lifts in this section will help you strengthen the lower back and buttocks. There is a specific five-step progression to these lifts, in which you move from double-leg to single-leg bridges.

Start by lying on your back on the floor or mat with your knees bent. Squeeze your butt and lift your hips up off the floor as far as you comfortably can. Aim to achieve a straight line from your shoulders to your knees. *Be careful not to arch your back.* Your knees should be bent to about 90 degrees or as much as comfortably possible.

Ch. 3 Fig. 35. Bridges/Hip Lifts Progression I

Hold the lift for 10 seconds and lower to the floor. Repeat 1–10 times.
When you have mastered the lift with both legs, try bringing one leg toward your chest. Make sure to keep your hips level while one leg is elevated. Lower the leg,

and then bring the opposite knee to your chest. Continue alternating sides, lowering your hips to rest as needed. Aim for good form.

Ch. 3 Fig. 36. Bridges/Hip Lifts Progression 2

Perform 1–30 repetitions on each side.

Ch. 3 Fig. 37. Bridges/Hip Lifts Progression 3

Once you have mastered bringing the knee to your chest, practice straightening one knee during the lift. Use your hands to help you extend and hold the leg or gently grasp behind your knee or calf.

Perform 1–30 repetitions on each side.

The next step in the progression is to eliminate the use of your hands to hold your leg up.

Perform 1–30 repetitions on each side.

Ch. 3 Fig. 38. Bridges/Hip Lifts Progression 4

The final step is to straighten your knee and hold your leg parallel with the opposite thigh. This is a very challenging exercise and may cause hamstring cramps. Take your time with the exercise and take rests as needed.

Quality is more important than quantity on this exercise. The goal is to be able to perform 1–30 repetitions.

Ch. 3 Fig. 39. Bridges/Hip Lifts Progression 5

## Quadruped Alternating Extension

The family dog or cat is an example of a quadruped, meaning that it moves on all four legs. Use this exercise to help strengthen your lower back and core.

Come down onto your hands and knees (quadruped position) on the floor or mat. Make sure that your knees are underneath your hips and your hands are underneath your shoulders. You can place a pillow or foam pad underneath your knees for support. Tighten your stomach muscles so that your back and neck are in a straight, neutral position. Your gaze should be down toward the floor.

Lift your left arm so that your thumb is pointed toward the ceiling. At the same time, extend the right leg backward. Imagine that you are reaching from the tips of your hand to the bottom of your foot. Keep your back, leg, and arm in a straight line—holding for 2–3 seconds before returning to your starting position. On the next repetition, lift your right arm and extend your left leg.

Perform 1–30 times on each side.

Ch. 3 Fig. 40. Quadruped Alternating Extension

## Front Planks

When done correctly, Front Planks are the ultimate core exercise. Come down onto your elbows and knees on the floor or mat. Bend your elbows, and rest your weight onto your forearms. Your hand position is self-selected. Straighten your legs out to create a straight line from your head to your heels. Do not elevate your hips. To keep your lower back from dropping or sagging, engage your stomach muscles as you hold the position. Keep your gaze toward the floor and do not let the head hang down. You may start on your knees if needed.

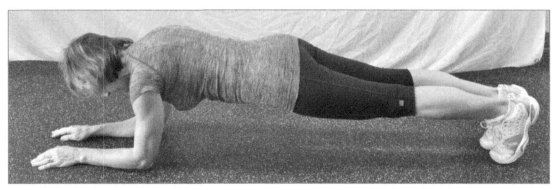

Ch. 3 Fig. 41. Front Plank

Start by holding for 5–10 seconds 5–10 times. Build yourself up to 1 minute holds for 3–10 repetitions interspersed throughout your workout.

## Side Planks

Side Planks are challenging and very effective at improving your trunk, hip, and shoulder stability. There are several variations of this plank for the beginner to the very advanced.

In this beginning slide plank, lie on your side on the floor or mat with your elbow directly under your shoulder. Your knees should be bent and stacked on top of one another. Bring your knees back so that they are in line with your hips, creating a straight line from your head to your knees. Engage your abdominal muscles and push up so that you are now weight bearing through your elbow and knees. Make sure you are also engaging (pushing) through your shoulders.

Ch. 3 Fig. 42. Beginning Side Plank

Work your way up to being able to hold the position for 10 seconds 10 times. You can progress by adding time and adjusting your repetitions accordingly. Once you have mastered this plank, you can go to the next difficulty level.

To increase the difficulty, extend the top leg.

Once you can hold the position for 10 seconds 10 times, progress by adding time and adjusting your repetitions accordingly.

When you are confident and comfortable, you can progress to the next level.

Ch. 3 Fig. 43. Side Plank with Top Leg Extended

To increase the difficulty, perform the straight leg version.

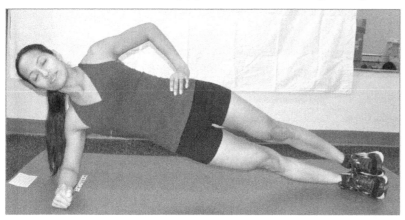

Once you can hold the position for 10 seconds 10 times, progress by adding time and adjusting your repetitions accordingly

When you are ready, you can progress to the next difficulty level.

Ch. 3 Fig. 44. Side Plank Straight Leg Version (Both Legs Extended)

**Note**: The straight leg position (both legs extended) can have several foot placement variations, depending on your balance and strength level.

To increase the challenge, progress toward having a straight elbow. Work your way up to being able to hold the position for 10 seconds 10 times. As with the two previous planks, progress by adding time and adjusting your repetitions accordingly.

One leg in front—or back—will help with the balance component.

Ch. 3 Fig. 45. Side Plank with Straight Elbow and Left Leg in Front

Ch. 3 Fig. 46. Side Plank Foot Placement Variation

Ch. 3 Fig. 47. Side Plank with Straight Elbow and Left Leg in Back

Make sure that you master this plank before moving to the next difficulty level. As you gain more confidence, work toward having your feet in a wider or stacked position. This makes the plank particularly challenging.

Practice until you can hold the position for 10 seconds 10 times before you add time and adjust your repetitions.

To progress to the next level of difficulty, perform the plank with one arm raised in the air.

Practice until you can hold the position for 10 seconds 10 times before adding time and adjusting repetitions.

Ch. 3. Fig. 48. Side Plank with Arm Raised

The next and final plank version is a very advanced maneuver. It may take months of solid repetition with earlier slide plank variations to achieve this level of stability. This progression takes time! While I encourage you to challenge yourself, make sure that you master each previous plank level before you progress to the next.

Once you are comfortable and confident—and only then—try the plank with an arm and leg raised in the air.

Ch. 3 Fig. 49. Side Plank with Leg and Arm Raised

## Squatting with a Band around Knees

Begin by placing an exercise band around your knees. Bring your feet about shoulder-width apart. Keep your knees in line with your toes. Begin to lower your buttocks toward the floor, keeping your knees apart and your trunk upright. Lower until your thighs are parallel to the floor. (If you feel as though you might fall, place a chair behind you for protection.) Pretend that you are about to sit down, but then stand up again. Keep your arms either stretched out in front, crossed over your chest, or overhead. The first of these is easiest and the last is the most difficult. The band will remind you to keep your knees over your toes and also help strengthen your hip abductor muscles.

Ch. 3. Fig. 50. Squatting with Band Around Knees Front View

Ch. 3. Fig. 51. Squatting with Band Around Knees Side View

Perform 1–30 times.

## Assisted Squats

To help you achieve more depth with your squat, it can be helpful to practice using assistance. Stand in front of a solid structure such as a railing, or even your kitchen sink. Perform the same squat as you did in the prior exercise, but this time aim for a deeper squat. Use the railing or sink for balance as you lower and raise yourself, but do not use it to pull yourself up. Assisted Squats can be performed with or without a band.

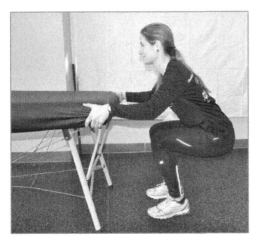

Ch. 3 Fig. 52. Assisted Squat

Ch. 3 Fig. 53. Assisted Squat with Band

Perform 1–30 times.

# Chapter 4: Enhancing Your Foundation

ᛞ Strive for progress, not perfection. ᛒ
—*Unknown*

This chapter contains the dynamic flexibility program I use with my clients. These movements are purposeful and organized in a specific manner designed to optimize muscle activation and mobility. You will notice that after some of the exercises, you are prompted to move directly to the next movement. With others, no such direction is provided. If I feel that an exercise outcome is more effective when performed as part of a series, it is made clear for you in the book.

As with all the exercises in this book, you should feel accomplished and not exhausted after a dynamic flexibility workout. Exhaustion is an indication that you may have overdone it. Continually overdoing it without the appropriate recovery can also lead to injury.

As you perform each of the dynamic flexibility movements in this chapter, your starting position will be the same unless otherwise noted.

You will start in an upright position with your head facing forward, chin level with the floor, and your feet shoulder-width apart. Place your hands at your sides with the palms facing toward your legs. This is referred to as the standard starting position. This will become second nature as you progress through the routine.

Enjoy your progress!

Ch. 4 Fig. 1. Standard Starting Position

**Exaggerated Marching**

Begin the Exaggerated Marching movement in the standard starting position.

Raise your left arm over your head, facing the head with your hand and fingers open. At the same time, raise the opposite (right) leg so the knee and thigh are now flexed as much as possible. From this position and staying within your comfort range, rise up onto your left toes.

Ch. 4 Fig. 2. Exaggerated Marching Right Leg

Step forward with the right leg. When your right foot touches the floor, lower your left arm back to your side.

Raise your right arm with the palm facing the head, hands and fingers open. At the same time, raise the left leg so the knee and thigh are hip height as you rise up onto your right toes.

Continue to march in a controlled and purposeful manner (one step at a time) 1–20 steps.

Ch. 4 Fig. 3. Exaggerated Marching Left Leg

## High Knee Low Knee

Begin the High Knee Low Knee exercise in the standard starting position. Raise your left arm over your head, facing the head with your hand and fingers open. At the same time, raise the opposite (right) leg so the knee and thigh are now flexed as much as possible. From this position, rise up onto your left toes as far as you can.

Reach down to the raised leg with your right hand to just below the knee and slide the hand down to your lower shin. Bring your heel toward your butt; your right heel should be nearly touching your butt. Then release the leg, step forward, and repeat with the opposite leg.

Continue the High Knee Low Knee in a controlled and purposeful manner 1–20 times.

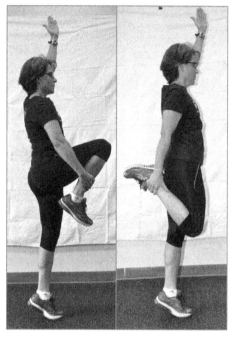

Ch. 4 Fig. 4. High Knee Low Knee Standard Version

If you have balance issues, do the modified flat foot version of this exercise.

Ch. 4 Fig. 5. High Knee Low Knee
Flat Foot Modification for Limited Balance

## Piriformis Walk

Begin the Piriformis Walk in the standard starting position. Raise your right arm over your head, facing the head with your hand and fingers open. Raise the right leg and bend your knee as you grasp your shin just above your ankle. Now pull your ankle toward your opposite hip. Continue gently supporting and lifting the leg as you rise up on the downward toes.

Release your leg from the position and take a step forward with it. Repeat this movement on the opposite side and perform 1–20 repetitions.

Ch. 4 Fig. 6. Piriformis Walk
Standard Version

Ch. 4 Fig. 7. Piriformis Walk
Modification for Balance with
Arm Down 1

Ch. 4 Fig. 8. Piriformis Walk
Modification for Balance with
Arm Down 2

## Windmill Walk

Start the Windmill Walk in the standard starting position. Raise your left arm over your head, facing the head with your hand and fingers open. Step forward with the opposite (right) leg approximately one step. When your right foot contacts the floor, reach down toward the right leg with the left hand, rotating from the hips and not bending the back. Reach as far as you comfortably can. For some, this may be your thigh. For others, this may be your toes.

Do not try to overreach the Windmill Walk. When your left hand reaches as far as it comfortably can—keeping your lower back flat—stand fully upright and repeat the exercise with the other side of your body.

Raise your right arm as you step forward with your left leg. Raise your right arm as high as possible. Now reach toward the left leg with the right hand, again rotating from the hips and not bending the back. Reach as far as you comfortably can. Now stand fully upright, and repeat the exercise on the other side of your body.

Perform the standard, beginner, and advanced versions of this exercise in the same manner.

Ch. 4 Fig. 9. Windmill Walk Standard Version

Do not rush this or any of the movements; maintain a controlled and purposeful pattern to your movement; stand fully upright between each Windmill Walk.

Repeat 1–20 times.

Ch. 4 Fig. 10. Windmill Walk Advanced Version

Ch. 4 Fig. 11. Windmill Walk Beginner Version

## Upright Windmill Walk

The Upright Windmill Walk involves the same hip flexion as the Windmill Walk. In this exercise, you touch your leg with the opposite hand while in an upright position. When doing this movement, resist kicking the leg, but instead lift to try to touch your toe. Overreaching can strain your back or legs. You may only be able to lift your leg a few inches to stay in your comfort zone.

Ch. 4 Fig. 12. Upright Windmill Walk

Begin the Upright Windmill Walk in the standard starting position. Raise your right arm up over your head, facing the head with your hand and fingers open. Lift the opposite (left) leg off the floor and bring the right hand to touch the left leg. Initially, you may only be able to touch your thigh or your knee. Over time, try to reach toward the toe but stay within your comfort zone. Lower the left leg and right arm to the side.

Repeat the movement for the right leg and left arm, performing 1–20 repetitions.

**Side Step with a Rear Crossover**

You will be moving from side to side in this movement. Adjust your position and environment accordingly and make sure you have enough room to do 1–20 side steps.

Begin this exercise in the standard starting position. Moving to your right, bring your left foot behind your right foot so that your little toe is next to your right heel. Your legs should be crossed. If your balance is challenged, modify your stance as necessary to stay safe. You may or may not feel a stretch in your left leg during this exercise. Keep your knees—which can be slightly bent—and toes facing forward and the hips squarely underneath the shoulders. To make this more challenging, simply take a larger step with your left leg.

Now step to your right with your right foot. Continue moving to the right and as you do, keep your hips, shoulders, and feet facing forward and your knees loose and not locked. Bring the left foot behind the right foot again, just as you did before.

Working with your balance and moving safely, try not to look down as you continue stepping to the right 1–20 times.

Ch. 4 Fig. 13. Side Step with a Rear Crossover Starting Position

Ch. 4 Fig. 14. Side Step with a Rear Crossover

**Tip**: Your hands can be in a self-selected position: on your hips, at your sides, or any position of comfort.

Now change direction and repeat the exercise on the opposite side. Moving to your left, bring your right foot behind your left foot so that your little toe is next to your left heel. Step to the left 1–20 times.

**Tip**: As with all dynamic flexibility exercises, you should not feel any discomfort. If you experience pain with this movement, stop and consult your healthcare provider.

### Upper Body Dynamic Flexibility Patterns Y.T.W.L.X.

The following Upper Body Dynamic Flexibility routine serves several purposes. Here, I am using it as a warmup to the remainder of the dynamic flexibility routine. These simple exercises also make an excellent office desk mini workout, precursor to a focused upper body exercise routine such as push-ups or pull-ups, or other purposeful body movements. They can also help you work on improving your upper body flexibility.

Use your arms to create the letters **Y**, **T**, **W**, **L**, and **X**. The focus of each of these letters is not on flailing arm movements, but rather on squeezing the shoulder blades down and back in a controlled and purposeful manner.

### Y

Begin the **Y** in the standard upright position. Raise both arms straight up over your head as far as you comfortably can. With your palms facing each other and fingers open, create an overhead **Y**.

Gently pull the shoulder blades down and back. Now, squeeze them together and release. Do not use your arms to force your shoulders backwards. Focus on achieving a smooth, purposeful, controlled backward motion in the shoulder blades. Repeat 1–20 times.

Ch. 4 Fig. 15. DFLEX Pattern Y Front and Back Views

**T**

After you complete **Y**, go directly to **T** of this Upper Body Dynamic Flexibility routine. Your arms are up and out to the sides at shoulder height, with your palms facing forward. Remember to keep the fingers open as in **Y**.

Using the same motion again, pull the shoulder blades backward, squeezing them down and back. Do not force the arms. Use your shoulder blades to perform the motion with control and purpose.

Repeat 1–20 times.

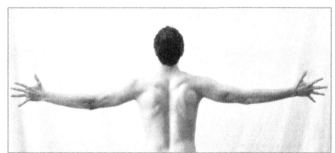

Ch. 4 Fig. 17. DFLEX Pattern T Back View

Ch. 4 Fig. 16. DFLEX Pattern T Front View

**W**

After you complete **T**, go directly to **W**. Bend and draw your elbows into the sides of the body toward your hips. Both arms together should now resemble the letter **W**. Keep your fingers open and palms facing forward.

As you did in **Y** and **T**, draw your shoulder blades backward, with a controlled and purposeful motion.

Repeat 1–20 times.

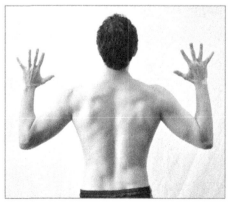

Ch. 4 Fig. 18. DFLEX Pattern W Front View

Ch. 4 Fig. 19. DFLEX Pattern W Back View

## L

From the **W** position, drop only the lower arms down so that they are parallel with the floor. Form an **L** on either side of your body. With your palms still forward and fingers open, repeat the backward shoulder blade squeeze as you have been doing with the other exercises in this Upper Body Dynamic Flexibility routine. Perform the **L** using the same controlled and purposeful technique. Repeat 1–20 times.

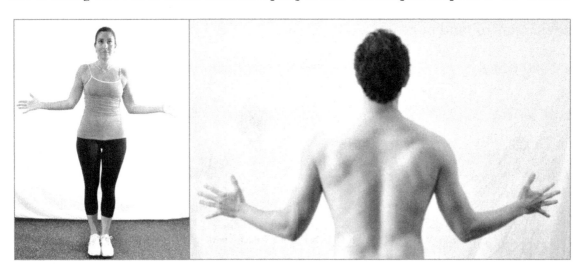

Ch. 4 Fig. 20. DFLEX Pattern L Front and Back Views

## X

From the **L** position, straighten both arms into the **T** position. Raise your right arm up and lower the left one down. Keep your palms facing forward and fingers open wide as you move the arms into a single-sided portion of an **X**. Repeat the backward shoulder blade squeeze as you have been doing in this section—maintaining your controlled and purposeful technique. After your repetitions, switch arms. Raise your left arm up and lower the right arm down. Keep your fingers open and palms facing forward. Repeat 1–20 times on each side for a total of no more than 40 repetitions.

Ch. 4 Fig. 21. DFLEX
Pattern X Front View

Ch. 4 Fig. 22. DFLEX Pattern X Back View

**Protraction Retraction (Push/Pull)**

This exercise employs the forward (protraction) and backward (retraction) movements of your shoulder blades. The only movement is the arms being pushed forward and pulled backward by the shoulder blades.

Begin this exercise in the standard starting position. Keep your chin, neck, and head in a neutral position throughout the movement. Do not shrug your shoulders. Raise your arms to shoulder height with the palms facing either the floor or each other. This is similar to the Frankenstein's monster position. Your raised arms should be level from the shoulders to the fingertips. Your shoulders should be relaxed and in line. Using only your shoulders, gently push your arms forward as far as you comfortably can, keeping them level with your shoulders. Round your shoulders forward while the rest of your back maintains its neutral position.

When you have reached the end point, begin retraction by pulling the shoulders back to their starting position. Continue to pull your arms backward until the shoulders are pulled back as far as is comfortably possible.

Ch. 4 Fig. 23. Push/Pull Protraction

Ch. 4 Fig. 24. Push/Pull Retraction

Ch. 4 Fig. 25. Push/Pull Protraction

Ch. 4 Fig. 26. Push/Pull Retraction

The shoulder blades have gone from fully forward to squeezed together. Continue this movement in a controlled, purposeful manner for a total of 1–20 repetitions.

## Jumpless Jack

For those of you who may remember the Jumping Jack—a gym class favorite, the Jumpless Jack is a similar but less jarring movement.

Begin the Jumpless Jack in the standard starting position. Raise your arms over your head as far as you comfortably can. At the same time you are raising your arms, rise up on your toes as far as you can.

You can interlace your fingers or thumbs overhead or keep your hands slightly apart. When you have reached the overhead position, try to reach a bit more for the ceiling and hold for 1–2 seconds. Gently lower the shoulders in a controlled manner, bringing your arms back down as you return to your starting position.

Repeat this movement 1–20 times.

Ch. 4 Fig. 27. Jumpless Jack Front View

Ch. 4 Fig. 28. Jumpless Jack Back View

## Balance Stands

The goal of the Balance Stands is to work the standing leg. In this exercise, you'll be moving one leg in three directions (forward, sideways, and backward), followed by the same sequence on the opposite leg. The moving leg provides the dynamic aspect of the exercise.

Begin the Balance Stand in the standard starting position. You may keep your hands on your hips or at your sides. Keep your right leg as straight as possible, but don't lock the knee. Now raise your right foot by moving it in a forward motion about 8–12 inches off the floor.

Ch. 4 Fig. 29. Balance Stand Leg Raise Front View

Try to maintain level hips throughout the movement. Your left standing leg should be straight but not locked. Bring the right foot back to the starting position and repeat this movement 1–20 times. Your balance should be challenged. That's a *good* thing!

**Tip**: To make the movement more difficult, keep your right foot from touching the floor as you bring it back and forth.

Ch. 4 Fig. 30. Balance Stand Leg Raise Side View

Now bring your right leg about 8–12 inches out to the side to continue working your left (standing) leg in a different dynamic direction.

Repeat this sideways movement with your right leg 1–20 times.

Ch. 4 Fig. 31. Balance Stand Leg Raise Back View

Change direction and bring your right (moving) leg backward 8–12 inches for 1–20 repetitions.

After completing 1–20 repetitions in all three directions (forward, sideways, and backward), you should feel the effort on the left standing leg.

Repeat the movement sequence on your other leg. The left leg is the moving leg and the right leg is the balance stand leg.

## Bobbing Bird

This exercise is a modification of the single leg dead lift. Begin the Bobbing Bird in the standard starting position. Raise both arms to shoulder-height with your palms facing each other or forward. You can raise your arms higher, but only if your comfort level allows. Pull the right leg backward, keeping your knee straight and right foot flexed. Continue bringing the right leg back as you rotate forward from the hips and reach your hands toward the floor simultaneously. You should be in a straight line from your head to your right foot throughout the movement.

You do not have to reach the floor; your goal is to rotate on the standing hip comfortably. If you must keep your hands above the knee to stay in your comfort level—because of a balance challenge or flexibility limitation—that's fine! Remember that you should not have pain during this or any exercise in this guide.

Ch. 4 Fig. 32. Bobbing Bird Arms at Shoulder Height

Ch. 4 Fig. 33. Bobbing Bird Downward End Point (with Hands Facing Back)

When you reach as far as you comfortably can, return to the starting position. Perform 1–20 repetitions on one leg, and then the other. Make a note to watch as you progress through several sessions to see how your balance and flexibility improve. This is progress!

As you perform the Bobbing Bird, work on your leg height, reaching your finger tips to the floor, and keeping your back straight.

Ch. 4 Fig. 34. Bobbing Bird Downward End Point (with Hands Facing Inward)

**Caution**: Bending over and standing up from this position can be challenging. If you feel dizzy or light-headed at any time during this exercise, stop and consult your healthcare provider before continuing.

## Step Overs

You will be moving from side to side in this movement. Adjust your position and environment accordingly and make sure you have enough room to do 1–20 side steps.

Begin the Step Overs movement in the standard starting position. Start by leading with the left leg. Raise your left knee as high as possible and then step over an imaginary wire. Raise your right leg and bring it up over the wire to meet your left leg. Your hands are in a self-selected position as you bring the feet from over the wire to the floor. Continue stepping to the left in the same manner 1–20 times.

Ch. 4 Fig. 35. Step Overs Leading with Left Leg (Over Imaginary Wire)

Now change direction. Using the same technique, step to the right 1–20 times.

As you perform these Step Overs, aim for leg height and good form.

Ch. 4 Fig. 36. Step Overs Leading with Right Leg (Over Imaginary Wire)

**Walking Lunge Series: Forward Walking Lunge**

Begin the Forward Walking Lunge in the standard starting position.

**Caution**: If you have a knee injury or limitation, be sure to stay within your comfort level during lunging. There should be no pain during this or any other dynamic flexibility exercise.

From your starting position, step forward with the right leg—a little longer than your normal step and bend the right knee. As you do so, lower the body downward. You do not need to lower all the way to the floor. *Keep your right (front) knee in line with and behind the middle toes of the right foot.* If you can tolerate bending to within a few inches off the floor, that is fine but not necessary. Try not to let the left knee touch the floor. When you reach your end point, come back up and step forward and through with your left leg. Try not to touch down with your left foot until it is in a fully forward position. Continue to "step, lunge, step, lunge" in a forward direction.

Ch. 4 Fig. 37. Forward Walking Lunge

Repeat this Forward Walking Lunge movement pattern 1–20 times, remembering to alternate legs.

Once you have completed this lunge and feel ready to progress, move on to the following Partial Sideways Walking Lunge.

**Walking Lunge Series: Partial Sideways Walking Lunge**

In this exercise, you will be moving from side to side. Adjust your position and environment accordingly and make sure you have enough room to do 1–20 side steps.

Begin in the standard starting position. Step to the left, keeping your feet straight ahead and toes pointed forward. Keep the toes in this position relative to the body throughout the movement.

Step sideways as far as you comfortably can. Shift your body weight onto your left (leading) knee. Do not let the left shoulder lean out beyond the left knee. Bend the left knee as if to partially sit on your left side. Keep your left knee in line and behind your toes. This bend is about half that of the Forward Walking Lunge. You should feel the sensation of effort in the left leg. The right (trailing) leg remains straight. In this stance, your feet remain pointed forward and flat on the floor. You should feel a slight stretch in your inner right thigh. Your hands and arms should be in a self-selected position. Now return to your starting position as you bring your right leg to your left leg.

Ch. 4 Fig. 38. Partial Sideways Walking Lunge Leading with Left Leg

Ch. 4 Fig. 39. Partial Sideways Walking Lunge Leading with Right Leg

Walk 1–20 steps to the left and then change your position. Now walk in the opposite direction—to the right 1–20 steps.

**Tip**: When doing these lunges, remember to keep your feet from rotating toward the movement. Practice using good form to get great results!

## Walking Lunge Series: Backward Walking Lunge

Now move on to the last, and most difficult, exercise of the three-way lunge set, the Backward Walking Lunge. It is difficult because you are not just moving backwards, but moving with limited vision. This lunge is in the opposite direction of the Forward Walking Lunge. Adjust your position and environment accordingly, making sure you have enough room to safely perform the movement.

**Caution**: Make sure that your path is clear to safely execute these backward lunges!

Begin the exercise in the standard starting position, with your arms in a self-selected stance.

Step backward with the right leg so that you're stepping back a little longer than your normal step. Bend both knees, bringing your right knee toward the floor. As your right knee moves down, slowly lower yourself downward. You should look as you did in the Forward Walking Lunge position.

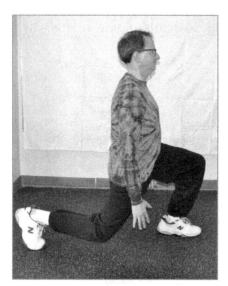

Rise up, remaining in the split-leg stance. Try to step backward and through with your left leg. If you need to half-step during this exercise to balance yourself, it's OK!

When the left leg is in position, begin the downward motion again with both legs. Do not hold the downward position. Rise up into the split stance position and continue your backward walking lunges.

Repeat 1–20 times.

Ch. 4 Fig. 40. Backward Walking Lunge

## Forward/Backward Assisted Leg Lift

Begin the Forward Assisted Leg Lift in the standard starting position. Lift your left knee. Your upper left leg and foot are level with the floor and your lower leg is perpendicular to the floor. Using both hands, lift the upper leg up and bring it toward your chest, grasping under your left thigh. At the same time, come up on the right toes. Now lower the left leg and as you do, take a step forward. Repeat the movement with the right leg for one repetition. Continue moving in a forward motion 1–20 times.

Now, change direction and do the Backward Assisted Leg Lift. Use the same technique to the point at which you lower your leg, but then step backward. Repeat the movement, alternating between each leg for one repetition. Continue moving in a backward motion 1–20 times.

**Caution**: Make sure you have sufficient room behind you and that your path is clear!

Ch. 4 Fig. 41. Forward/Backward Assisted Leg Lift

## Double-Handed Overhead Leg Lift

The Double-Handed Overhead Leg Lift is similar to the Upright Windmill Walk (on page 84) and requires the same precautions. In this exercise, you have the option of performing these leg lifts either by moving forward or standing in place.

Begin the Double-Handed Overhead Leg Lift in the standard starting position.

Raise both arms together and join your hands in front of you. If you are able to tolerate raising your arms over your head, do so.

Ch. 4 Fig. 42. Double-Handed Overhead Leg Lift

Lift your right leg as far as you comfortably can. Avoid kicking the leg up. Slightly flex the knee and foot, positioning the toes toward your nose. Bring your hands down to touch your elevated right leg. You need not lift it higher than your hip. If you raised your hands to chest height (and not over your head), keep them there.

Ch. 4 Fig. 43. Double-Handed Overhead Lift (Right Leg Elevated)

Ch. 4 Fig. 44. Double-Handed Overhead Lift (Arms Re-elevated While Lowering Leg)

Ch. 4 Fig. 45. Double-Handed Overhead Lift (Returning Leg to Floor)

When you reach the end point of your leg lift, return your arms to chest height or overhead, depending on the position you selected. Lower the leg in a controlled, purposeful manner (do not drop the leg) and either step forward with the right leg or return to your starting position. Repeat the movement, alternating between each leg for one repetition.

Perform 1–20 times.

## Dynamic Global Side Step

There are three distinct leg movements per repetition of the Dynamic Global Side Step. In this exercise, you have the option of performing your side steps either standing in place or moving sideways for a more dynamic effect. If you choose the dynamic method, adjust your position and environment accordingly to allow enough room to do 1–20 side steps.

Begin in the standard starting position. Your hands are in a self-selected stance. Raise both arms so that your elbows are shoulder height. Position your lower arms perpendicular to the floor, with your fingertips pointed toward the ceiling. Face both palms forward and keep your fingers spread wide. This is the goal post stance. If the goal post position is too difficult, choose a self-select arm position.

First, raise and bend your left knee forward, but no higher than your hip. Now lower the leg as you return your left foot to the floor. Your legs are in your starting position with your arms still in the goal post stance.

Ch. 4 Fig. 46. Dynamic Global Side Step 1 (Goal Post Stance)

Ch. 4 Fig. 47. Dynamic Global Side Step (Left Leg Lift with Bent Knee)

Ch. 4 Fig. 48. Dynamic Global Side Step (Return to Goal Post Stance)

Next, raise the left leg again, no higher than your hip and without bending the knee. Control the movement; it is not a kick, but rather a controlled and purposeful lift. We know that your arms are becoming fatigued as you maintain the goal post stance! Now, without dropping the leg, lower it to the floor in a controlled, purposeful manner. Try to maintain good form.

Ch. 4 Fig. 49. Dynamic Global Side Step 2 (Left Leg Lift with Straight Knee)

Ch. 4 Fig. 50. Dynamic Global Side Step (Return to Goal Post Stance)

Finally, lift the left leg out to the side so that your left leg meets your left elbow. Here, you are bending the left knee and turning it toward your left shoulder. Keep the inner leg and bent knee facing forward as you raise the leg as high as you comfortably can. (Use your elbow height to gauge how high you can raise your leg.)

Ch. 4 Fig. 51. Dynamic Global Side Step 3 (Left Leg Lift to Side)

Ch. 4 Fig. 52. Dynamic Global Side Step (Return to Goal Post)

Ch. 4 Fig. 53. Dynamic Global Side Step (Dynamic Method)

If you are performing your steps in place, bring your left leg to your starting position and complete the same movements with the right leg. Continue alternating between legs 1–20 repetitions.

If you are stepping sideways—using the dynamic method, take a step to the left. (Do not return to the standard starting position.) Repeat the movement with the right leg. Continue alternating between legs 1–20 repetitions.

## Floor Ladder Crawl

In the Floor Ladder Crawl, you will be moving forward on the floor as you climb an imaginary ladder. To prepare for this exercise, adjust your space accordingly before you begin.

Start by getting into a push-up position on the floor or mat. Your hands are shoulder-width; you are on your toes; your body weight is on your hands and feet; and you are looking at the floor.

From this position, reach as far forward on the floor as you comfortably can with your right arm. With the arm extended, picture yourself grabbing for the first rung of the ladder. Bring your left knee up toward your left elbow alongside your body as you get footing on another rung of your ladder. Next, reach as far as you comfortably can with your left arm and grab for the next rung of the ladder. Then bring your right knee up toward your right elbow alongside your body as you get footing on another rung of your ladder.

Ch. 4 Fig. 54. Floor Ladder Crawl

Continue the movement, fluidly reaching and stepping simultaneously as you climb your floor ladder.

Perform 1–20 repetitions in a controlled, purposeful manner.

As you become more accomplished, you can reach farther and farther. Unlike a real ladder, you don't have to worry about falling too far! For added fun, when you have reached the end, try climbing backward down the ladder. You should find this equally as challenging.

## Inchworm

Begin the Inchworm in the standard starting position. Hinge forward from the hip and lower your hands to the floor. As you do so, bend your knees slightly, put your head between the upper arms, and look toward your feet.

With your hands on the floor, walk them out away from your body, keeping your arms approximately shoulder-width apart. Get as close to a push-up position as you can tolerate. Be careful not to overreach your arms. Keep your stomach pulled in and your back flat.

When you have reached your end point, your hands should be under your shoulders or slightly in front of them. Try not to rest your knees on the floor, but it's OK if you need a mini break. Begin to tiptoe your feet toward your hands. As your butt lifts higher, you should look like an inchworm. (This is similar to the downward dog position in yoga.)

When you reach your end point, you should feel a slight stretch in the lower back and behind the legs—from your hips through your heels. This is one repetition.

Continue moving forward in this fashion 1–20 times.

Ch. 4 Fig. 55. Inchworm Steps 1-5

**Sideways Crawl**

The Sideways Crawl will be done moving sideways, so you'll want to adjust your exercise space accordingly before you begin.

Begin by getting onto your hands and knees into a crawl position on the floor or mat. Your hands are underneath the shoulders and knees under the hips.

Ch. 4 Fig. 56. Sideways Crawl Side View

Ch. 4 Fig. 57. Sideways Crawl Front View

From this position move your left knee and hand out to the left simultaneously, away from your body. Keep the knee and hand at the same distance from your core. Once your left hand and knee reach their end point—staying within your comfort zone, lower them to the floor. This zone could be from 1–6 inches. You are now back in your starting crawl position. Follow with the right hand and knee. Using this technique, continue moving to the left and crawl 1–20 times.

Ch. 4 Fig. 58. Sideways Crawl Side View (with Left Knee and Hand Out to Side simultaneously)

Ch. 4 Fig. 59. Sideways Crawl Side View (with Left Knee and Hand Returning to Crawl Position)

Repeat the movement in the opposite direction. Crawl to the right 1–20 times.

**Moving Front Plank**

This movement is done moving sideways. As with the Sideways Crawl, make sure you give yourself enough room to maneuver before you begin. The Moving Front Plank is a very challenging exercise! If this is too strenuous for you, the Sideways Crawl is an excellent substitute.

Start by getting into a push-up position on the floor or mat. Your hands are shoulder-width; you are on your toes; your body weight is on your hands and feet; and you are looking at the floor.

From this position, move your left arm and leg out to the left at the same time, aligning them the same distance from your core. If your plank position is uneven or you are uncomfortable, move the arm first and then the leg. You can move just a few inches at a time until you learn what is comfortable.

Continue moving sideways to the left in this fashion until you have completed 1–20 repetitions. When done, take a mini break if you need one. Now repeat the movement in the opposite direction 1–20 repetitions.

Ch. 4 Fig. 60. Moving Front Plank

**Roll Up Series: Front Roll Up**

The goals of the Roll Up Series are to engage your abdominals, increase your hamstring flexibility, and develop your hip range of motion (ROM).

Start the Front Roll Up by sitting on your butt with your knees bent and your hands either in front of or behind your knees. Pull your stomach in toward your spine. Begin to roll one vertebra at a time onto your back, pulling your knees toward your chest. Immediately roll back up—one vertebra at a time—onto your butt again. While momentum is helpful in this activity, the roll up is more about control than speed. Perform 1–20 times.

When performing all roll ups, remember to:

- Keep your butt on the floor or mat.
- Avoid rolling up onto your shoulders.
- Keep from rolling up so far that you roll back on your head or lift the middle of your back off the floor.
- Maintain control throughout the movement.

**Note**: Remember to roll one vertebra at a time in both directions.

Ch. 4 Fig. 61. Roll Up Preparations (Without Leg Extension) Steps 1-5

It is suggested that you proceed directly to the next movement in this series, the Figure 4 Roll Up.

### Figure 4 Roll Up

Begin as you did in the previous roll up. Instead of rolling back onto your butt, unbend from the knees and fluidly straighten your left leg as you lower it to the floor.

While lowering the straightened left leg, maintain a right bent knee and place the sole of your right foot toward the inside of the left leg. The position of your foot against the inside of the leg depends on your comfort level. Your legs should resemble the figure 4. Now reach toward your left leg with both hands. Once you have reached your end point, begin to roll back, bringing both knees toward your chest as you return to your starting position.

On the second repetition, keep your left (opposite) leg bent as you fluidly straighten your right leg, lowering it to the floor in front of your butt. This is a fluid movement from rolling back to the figure 4 position. Continue alternating 1–20 times.

Ch. 4 Fig. 62. Figure 4 Roll Up Steps 1-3

It is suggested that you go straight to the next movement in this series, the Butterfly Roll Up.

## Butterfly Roll Up

Once you have completed 1–20 repetitions of the Figure 4 Roll Up, continue with the Butterfly Roll Up.

Begin as you did in the Front Roll Up. Instead of rolling back onto your butt, unbend from the knees and begin to straighten the legs, but not completely. Keep the knees partially bent and let the outsides of your legs lower toward the floor, keeping the soles of your feet together. Picture your legs resembling the forewings of a butterfly.

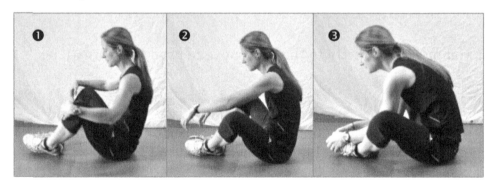

Ch. 4 Fig. 63. Butterfly Roll Up

Now lean forward with your body to its end point and roll back, bringing your knees to your chest as in the previous roll ups. Repeat this movement 1–20 times.
I suggest that you go straight to the next exercise in this series, the Straight Leg Roll Up.

## Straight Leg Roll Up

Once you have completed 1–20 repetitions of the Butterfly Roll Up, continue with the Straight Leg Roll Up.

Begin as you did in the Front Roll Up. Instead of rolling back onto your butt, straighten both legs and reach for your toes. When you reach your end point, roll back and bring your knees to your chest as in the previous roll ups. Keep your stomach tight as you perform this movement. Repeat 1–20 times.

Ch. 4 Fig. 64. Straight Leg Roll Up Steps 1-4

It is suggested that you go straight to the final exercise in this series, the Split Leg Roll Up.

## Split Leg Roll Up

Once you have completed 1–20 repetitions of the Straight Leg Roll Up, complete the series with the Split Leg Roll Up.

Begin as you did in the Front Roll Up. Roll out by bringing your legs straight out, but in a V pattern. As you let the knees straighten in front of you, reach forward between the legs as far as you comfortably can.

When you reach your end point, roll back to your starting position as in the previous roll ups for one repetition. Repeat 1–20 times.

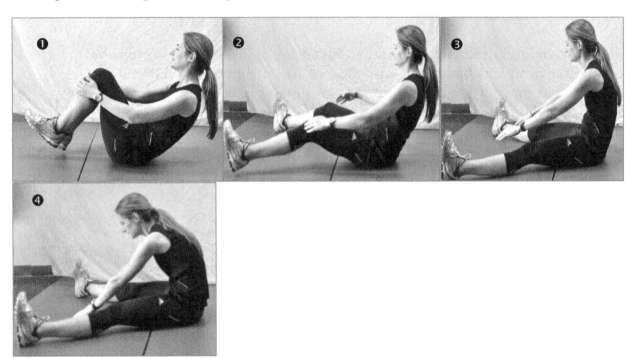

Ch. 4 Fig. 65. Split Leg Roll Up Steps 1-4

## Toe/Heel Walks Series: Forward/Backward Toe Walk

The Toe/Heel Walk Series begins with the Forward Toe Walk. Start in the standard starting position. Rise up onto your toes to your comfort level. This doesn't have to be on tiptoe. A slight heel elevation is OK. Walk forward on your toes with your knees slightly bent. Keep your torso upright, feet shoulder-width apart, and chin level with the floor.

Move your arms and hands as you would during normal walking. Take 1–20 steps.

Ch. 4 Fig. 66. Forward Toe Walk

Once you have completed the Forward Toe Walk, proceed directly to the Backward Toe Walk. The Backward Toe Walk is the same movement as the Forward Toe Walk, but in reverse. If you need to rest between movements, that is fine.

This can be challenging because moving backwards is generally a difficult task. Take 1–20 steps.

Ch. 4 Fig. 67. Backward Toe Walk

**Caution**: Make sure your path is clear before you do this exercise! Even while you are proceeding in reverse, glance back occasionally to ensure that your exercise path remains clear.

### Forward/Backward Heel Walk

Begin in the standard starting position. Now raise the toes so that you are on your heels. This may feel awkward and unbalanced. The toes need only be slightly off the floor to be effective. Begin walking forward. Try to look forward. Remember to take a break if you feel you need one. Take 1–20 steps.

As you did with the previous toe walks, now take 1–20 steps backwards.

Ch. 4 Fig. 68. Backward Heel Walk

Ch. 4 Fig. 69. Backward Heel Walk

## Side Toe Walk

As the name implies and just like the Forward Toe Walk, you will be moving on your toes again. You will be moving to the side, so adjust yourself in your environment appropriately.

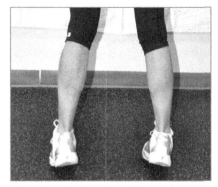

Ch. 4 Fig. 70. Side Toe Walk

As with the Forward Toe Walk, start in the standard starting position. When raised on the toes, begin to walk sideways 1–20 steps. Be aware of your surroundings and make sure your path is clear. Remember to keep your feet from rotating toward the movement direction. When you have walked 1–20 steps, return to the same start and walk 1–20 steps in the opposite direction.

## Side Heel Walk

To perform the Side Heel Walk, elevate the toes and stand up on your heels. Start in the standard starting position, but this time you begin *on your heels*.

Begin sidestepping on your heels 1–20 steps. As you step, keep your feet straight under your legs and from rotating toward the movement direction. When you have sidestepped 1–20 steps in one direction, sidestep 1–20 steps back to your starting Side Heel Walk position.

Congratulations on completing the Toe/Heel Walks Series.

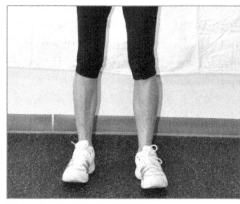

Ch. 4 Fig. 71. Side Heel Walk

# Chapter 5: Assessment Express℠
## Finding Your Trouble Spots

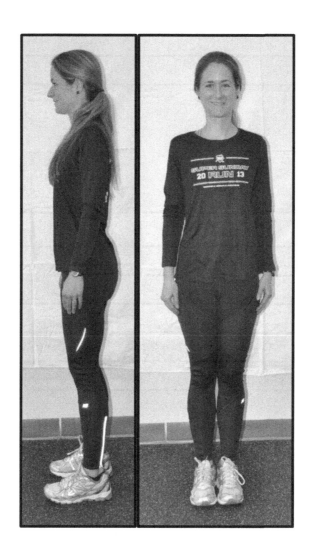

**Neck Flexion**

Page 20

**Notes:**

_____
_____
_____
_____
_____

**Neck Rotation
(Right & Left)**

Pages 20-21

**Notes:**
_____

**Right**
_____
_____
_____

**Left**
_____
_____
_____

**Neck Extension**

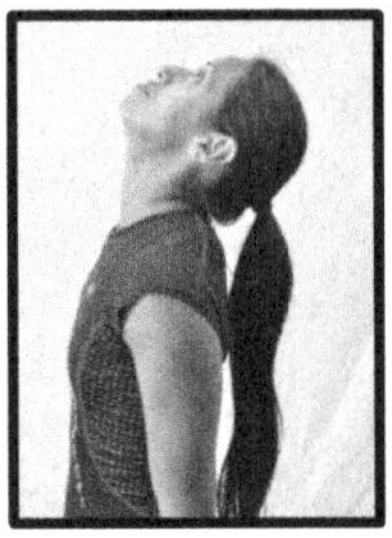

Pages 21-22

**Notes:**

_____
_____
_____
_____
_____

**Upper Back Scratch
(Right & Left)**

Pages 25-26

**Notes:** _____

**Right** _____

_____

_____

**Left** _____

_____

_____

**Lower Back Scratch
(Right & Left)**

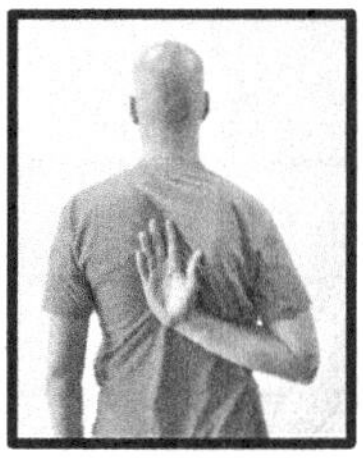

Page 32

**Notes:** _____

**Right** _____

_____

_____

**Left** _____

_____

_____

**Upper Back Scratch
(Prone–Right & Left)**

Page 26

**Notes:** _____

**Right** _____

_____

_____

**Left** _____

_____

_____

## Shoulder Flexion
## (Prone–Right & Left)

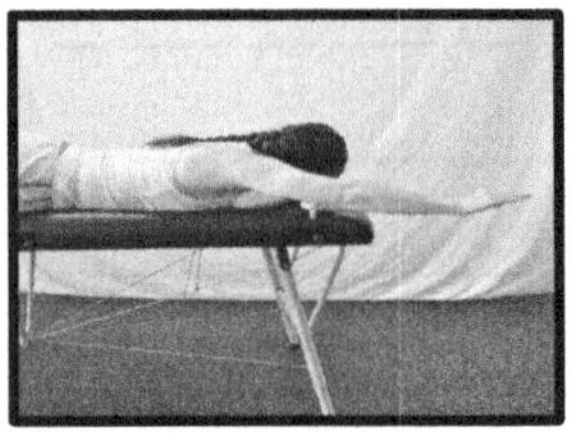

Pages 26-27

**Notes:** _____

**Right** _____

_____

_____

**Left** _____

_____

_____

## Shoulder External
## Rotation
## (Prone–Right & Left)

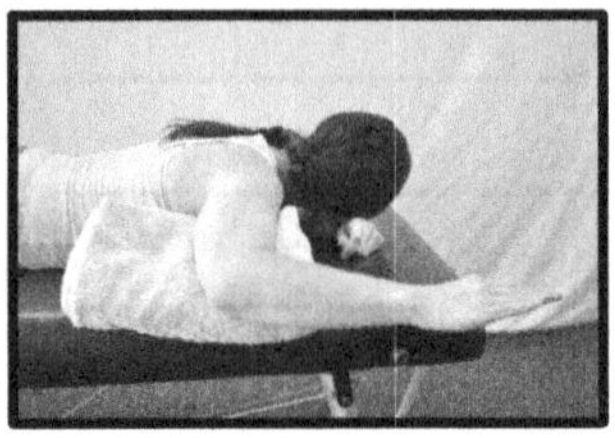

Pages 26-27

**Notes:** _____

**Right** _____

_____

_____

**Left** _____

_____

_____

## Lower Back Scratch
## (Prone–Right & Left)

Page 33

**Notes:** _____

**Right** _____

_____

_____

**Left** _____

_____

_____

**Shoulder Extension
(Prone–Right & Left)**

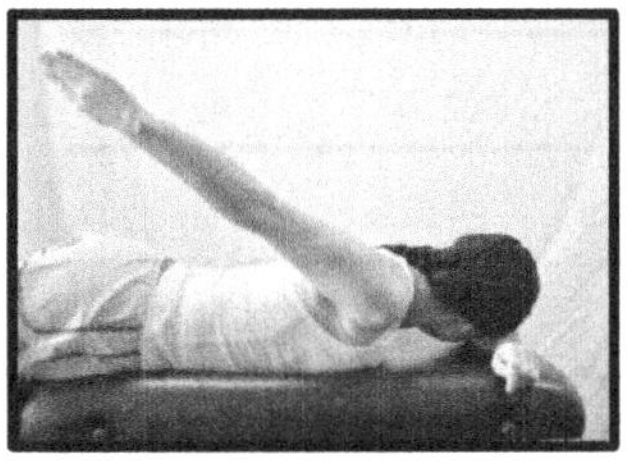

Page 33

**Notes:** _____

**Right** _____

_____

_____

**Left** _____

_____

_____


**Shoulder Internal
Rotation
(Prone–Right & Left)**

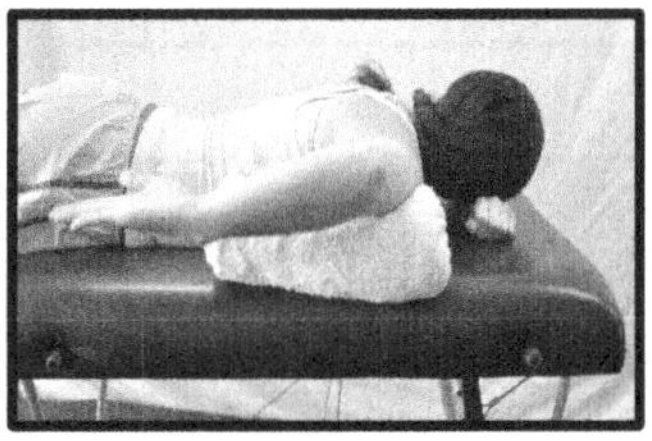

Page 34

**Notes:** _____

**Right** _____

_____

_____

**Left** _____

_____

_____


**Thoracic Spine Rotation
(Right & Left)**

Page 29

**Notes:** _____

**Right** _____

_____

_____

**Left** _____

_____

_____

## Prone Press Up

Page 37

**Notes:**
_____
_____
_____
_____
_____

## Child's Pose

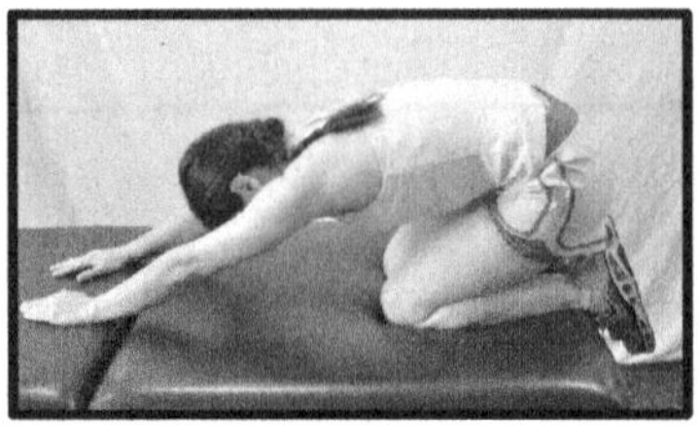

Page 43

**Notes:**
_____
_____
_____
_____
_____

## Shoulder Flexion (Supine)

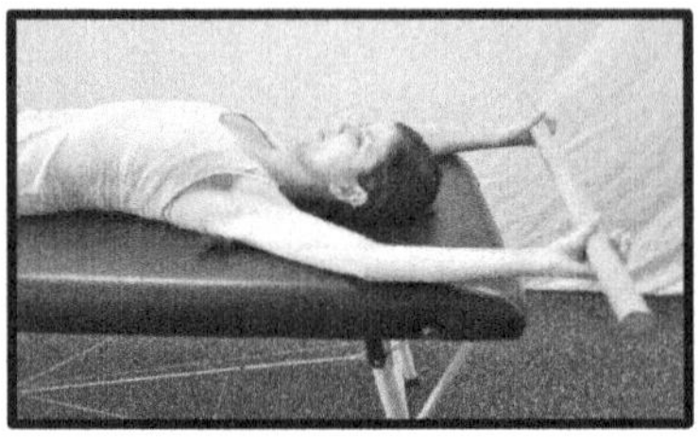

Page 28

**Notes:**
_____
_____
_____
_____
_____

**Straight Leg Raise
(Right & Left)**

Page 44

**Notes:** _____

**Right** _____

_____

_____

**Left** _____

_____

_____

**Leg Extension
(Right & Left)**

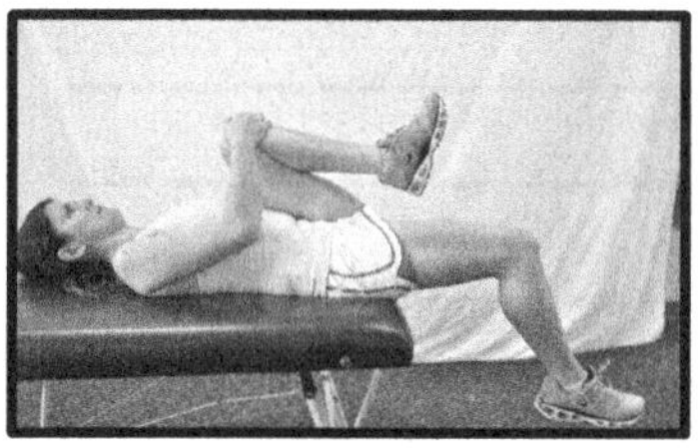

Page 39

**Notes:** _____

**Right** _____

_____

_____

**Left** _____

_____

_____

**Forward Bend**

Page 43

**Notes:** _____

_____

_____

_____

_____

## Whole Body
## Extension

Page 37

**Notes:**

_____

_____

_____

_____

_____

## Overhead Squat

Page 47

**Notes:**

_____

_____

_____

_____

_____

## Overhead Squat
## (Side View)

Page 47

**Notes:**

_____

_____

_____

_____

_____

**Modified Overhead Squat**     **Notes:**

Page 48

_____

_____

_____

_____

_____

**Ankle Mobility
(Right & Left)**     **Notes:**

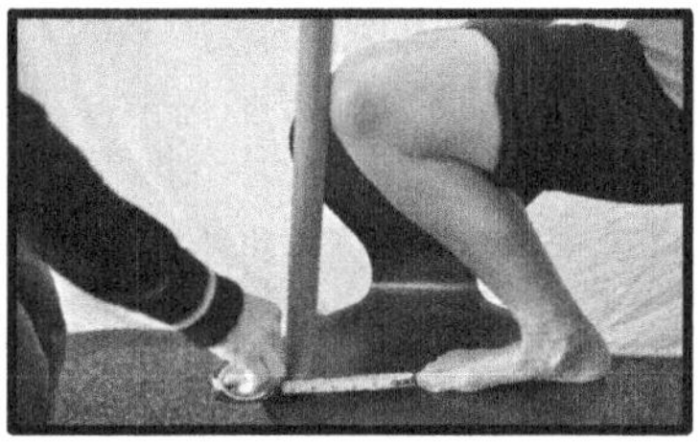

Page 49

**Right** _____

_____

_____

**Left** _____

_____

_____

**Single Leg Balance
(Right & Left)**     **Notes:**

Page 50

**Right** _____

_____

_____

**Left** _____

_____

_____

# Chapter 6: Final Thoughts

৪৩ Think about the way you exercise. It should follow the way you were designed to move. It should make sense. It should be purposeful. You should enjoy it and be able to perform it forever. ೞ

In this book, you have been able to look at your movement patterns in order to determine if you are fit at the basic functional movement level. You have also been provided with a system of specific exercises to:

- Help correct any limitations you may have, and

- Maintain normal strength, flexibility, mobility, balance, and stability.

Whether you are an athlete or just looking for an effective, simple and fun workout routine, this proven exercise modality can be used for life.

My hope is that you have come to understand the two main differences between this book and most other fitness books. First, the dynamic flexibility program can be implemented by almost anyone, regardless of age or fitness level. Whether a client is an elite athlete or one with a visual or other physical impairment, this program consistently produces excellent results. This success over time is directly related to the primary goal, which has always been to keep you moving well.

What also distinguishes this book is the functional movement self-assessment provided in Chapter 2. You now know how to find your challenges so that you can become fit at a foundational level. You can also use the self-assessment results to guide your own exercise program as you progress.

## Remembering the Basics

To maximize your time and effort, it is imperative that you use this guide as outlined. Use Chapter 2 to find and record those trouble spots. Then choose the exercises in Chapters 3 and 4 to help you reduce those limitations. Keep in mind that if you work only on the easy exercises, you will not make sufficient progress toward normal functional movement.

Effecting change and making progress are difficult initially, but the results are worth it. My clients often tell me: "I feel better." "I move better." "I'm less stiff." "My back doesn't hurt anymore."

While dynamic flexibility may not solve all your aches and pains, it has helped so many clients improve their daily functioning and athletic pursuits. Just like an infant has to learn to roll over before it can sit up, so too every person should master basic functional movement before participating in vigorous activity.

## Managing Your Success

Now that you have taken these important steps to become fit at the foundational level, I suggest that you make dynamic flexibility part of your weekly exercise routine. While it can be performed daily, a dynamic flexibility routine at least 2–3 times per week is sufficient for most people. And for some, this will be enough exercise, period. For others who participate in specific activities such as running, cycling, golf, and so on, dynamic flexibility is the cornerstone of a well-rounded fitness program.

Once you have mastered the program, you can use it to maintain your fitness level. Try doing a few of the exercises as a warmup before any activity, and a full DFLEX routine 1–2 times per week. All of the dynamic flexibility exercises in Chapter 4 can be performed in approximately 60 minutes.

Do *not* rush or feel any pressure to accomplish a full routine in 60 minutes. For starters, you may be moving slower on some days than on others. You may also decide to focus on a particular set of challenging exercises on a given day, rather than on an entire routine. Do what feels good to you. Concentrate on your form and move in a controlled, purposeful manner, knowing that we all progress through these exercises at our own pace. Every 2–4 weeks or so, revisit the Functional Movement Self-Assessment or use the Assessment Express to see how you actually progress.

I hope that this guide has given you the tools you need to exercise safely, effectively, purposefully, and for life. When we move better, we feel better. We can perform our daily and sporting activities with greater confidence and fluidity. Dynamic flexibility has transformed not only my clients, but myself. Namaste.

# Bibliography

Allison, Sarah J., David M. Bailey, and Jonathan P. Folland. "Prolonged Static Stretching Does not Influence Running Economy Despite Changes in Neuromuscular Function." *Journal of Sports Sciences* 26, no. 14 (December 2008): 1489–1495.

Bordoni, Bruno, and Marta Simonelli. "The Awareness of the Fascial System." *Cureus*, 10, no. 10 (October 2018): e3397. doi:10.7759/cureus.3397.

Bridewell, Keith. "Ligaments." *SpineUniverse*. Updated April 10, 2018. https://www.spineuniverse.com/anatomy/ligaments.

Burfoot, Amby. "The 10-Percent Rule." *Runners' World*, November 14, 2001. http://www.runnersworld.com/running-tips/the-10-percent-rule.

Cook, Gray. *Athletic Body in Balance*. Chicago: Human Kinetics, 2003.

Covert, Christoper A., Melanie P. Alexander, John J. Petronis, and Scott D. Davis. "Comparison of Ballistic and Static Stretching on Hamstring Muscle Length Using an Equal Stretching Dose." *Journal of Strength and Conditioning Research* 24, no. 11 (November 2010): 3008–3014. doi:10.1519/jsc.0b013e3181bf3bb0.

Davies, Clair, and Amber Davies, *The Trigger Point Therapy Workbook*, Third Edition. Oakland: New Harbinger Publications, Inc., 2013.

Eveleigh, Janice. "Dynamic Stretching." *Stretching-Exercises-Guide*. http://www.stretching-exercises-guide.com/dynamic-stretching.html.

Fradkin, Andrea J., C. A. Sherman, and C. F. Finch. "Improving Golf Performance with a Warmup Conditioning Program." *British Journal of Medicine* 38, no. 6 (December 2004): 762–765. doi:10.1136/bjsm.2003.009399.

Garber, Carol Ewing, Bryan Blissmer, Michael R. Deschenes, Barry A. Franklin, Michael J. Lamonte, I-Min Lee, David C. Nieman, and David P. Swain. "American College of Sports Medicine position stand. Quantity and Quality of Exercise for Developing and Maintaining Cardiorespiratory, Musculoskeletal, and Neuromotor Fitness in Apparently Healthy Adults: Guidance for Prescribing Exercise." *Medicine and Science in Sports and Exercise* 43, no. 7 (2011): 1334–1359.

Haddad, Monoem, Amir Dridi, Moktar Chtara, Anis Chaouachi, Del P. Wong, David Behm, and Karim Chamari. "Static Stretching Can Impair Explosive Performance for at Least 24 Hours." *Journal of Strength and Conditioning Research* 28, no. 1 (January 2014): 3008–3014. doi:10.1519 /jsc.0b013e3182964836.

Holt, B. W., and K. Lambourne. "The Impact of Different Warm-Up Protocols on Vertical Jump Performance in Male Collegiate Athletes." *Journal of Strength and Conditioning Research* 22, no. 1 (January 2008): 226–229. doi:10.1519 /jsc.0b013e31815f9d6a.

Kendall, Florence P., and Elizabeth Kendall McCreary. *Muscles: Testing and Function.* 4th ed. Baltimore: Williams and Wilkins, 1983.

Lindquist, Barb. "Dynamic Mobility Drills." (Handout received in Olympian Barb Lindquist Triathlon Clinic with Coach Barb Lindquist, Germantown, PA, March 23, 2019.)

Lowery, Ryan P., Jordan M. Joy, Lee E. Brown, Eduardo O. de Souza, David R. Wistocki, Gregory S. Davis, Marshall A. Naimo, Gina A. Zito, and Jacob M. Wilson. "Effects of Static Stretching on 1 Mile Uphill Run Performance." *Journal of Strength and Conditioning Research* 28, no. 1 (January 2014): 161–167. doi:10.1519/jsc.0b013e3182956461.

Magee, David J. *Orthopedic Physical Assessment.* St. Louis: Elsevier / Saunders, 2008.

McLarty, Sara, and Misty Becerra. "Swimming Technique and Training." In *USA Triathlon Level 1 Coaching Certification Manual.* Colorado Springs: USA Triathlon, 2011.

Moore, Keith L., Arthur F. Dalley, and Anne M. R. Agur. *Clinically Oriented Anatomy.* 6th ed. Baltimore: Lippencott Williams and Wilkins, 2010.

Moroz, Alex. "Physical Therapy (PT)." *Merck Manual for the Professional.* Updated June, 2017. https://www.merckmanuals.com/professional/special-subjects /rehabilitation/physical-therapy-pt.

Neumann, Donald A. *Kinesiology of the Musculoskeletal System: Foundations for Rehabilitation.* St. Louis: Elsevier / Mosby, 2009.

Page, Phil. "Current Concepts in Muscle Stretching for Exercise and Rehabilitation." *International Journal of Sports Physical Therapy* 7, no. 1 (February 2012): 109–119.

Ryan, Eric D., Travis W. Beck, Trent J. Herda, Holly R. Hull, Michael J. Hartman, Pablo B. Costa, Jason M. Defreitas, Jeffery R. Stout, and Joel T. Cramer. "The Time Course of Musculotendinous Stiffness Responses Following Different Durations of Passive Stretching." *Journal of Orthopaedic & Sports Physical Therapy®*, 38, no. 10 (October 2008): 632–639.

Reynolds, Gretchen. *The First Twenty Minutes*. New York: Penguin, 2013. See esp. chap. 2, "Stretching The Truth."

Thompson, Walter R. "Worldwide Survey of Fitness Trends for 2019." *American College of Sports Medicine's Health & Fitness Journal* 22, no. 6 (November/December 2018): 10–17. doi: 10.1249/FIT.0000000000000438.

Wilson, Jacob M., Lyndsey M. Hornbuckle, Jeong-Su Kim, Carlos Ugrinowitsch, Sang-Rok Lee, Michael C. Zourdoa, Brian Sommer, and Lynn B. Panton. "Effects of Static Stretching on Energy Cost and Running Endurance Performance." *Journal of Strength and Conditioning Research* 24, no. 9 (September 2010): 2274–2279. doi:10.1519/jsc.0b013e3181b22ad6.

# Index

# About the Author

**Rod Murray**, EP-C, CIFT, LMT, RYT, has been a health and fitness professional for more than 35 years. He attended the U.S. Naval Submarine School and Naval School of Health Sciences. Rod served as a Navy Corpsman with the Navy and Marine Corps and was also a Medic with the Army National Guard. After his military service, he studied biology, nuclear medicine, health physics, and massage therapy at County College of Morris, Manhattan College, St. Joseph's School of Nuclear Medicine, and The Institute for Therapeutic Massage. He also attended Columbia University while on staff as a member of the Office of Radiation Safety.

Coach Rod currently owns Body4Life Training in Morristown, NJ, and works as an ACSM Certified Exercise Physiologist (EP-C), Certified Inclusive Fitness Trainer (CIFT), and Licensed Massage Therapist (LMT). He is a USA Cycling Level 1 (expert level) coach and USA Weightlifting coach. Rod is a USA Cycling Category 1 mountain bike racer, and also the event director for Girls Guts Glory hike / bike / run in Morristown, NJ. Rod established Girls Guts Glory in 2014 to benefit The Mental Health Association of Essex and Morris counties. In 2019, Rod earned the distinction of Registered Yoga Teacher (RYT) by Yoga Alliance®, the largest nonprofit representing the yoga community.

Made in the USA
Middletown, DE
12 February 2020